Power and Tactics in International Negotiation

William Mark Habeeb

POWER AND TACTICS
IN
INTERNATIONAL
NEGOTIATION

How Weak Nations Bargain with
Strong Nations

The Johns Hopkins University Press
Baltimore and London

The Johns Hopkins University Press
701 West 40th Street
Baltimore, Maryland 21211
The Johns Hopkins Press Ltd., London

The paper used in this publication meets the minimum requirements of
American National Standard for Information Sciences—Permanence of Paper
for Printed Library Materials, ANSI Z39.48-1984.

Library of Congress Cataloging-in-Publication Data

Habeeb, William Mark, 1955–
    Power and tactics in international negotiation.

    Bibliography: p.
    Includes index.
    1. Diplomatic negotiations in international disputes.
2. Balance of power.   I. Title.
JX4473.H33   1988   327.2   87-46307
ISBN 0-8018-3620-4 (alk. paper)

To My Parents and Mimi

Contents

vii

CONTENTS

Preface and Acknowledgments

This book is a study of power in asymmetrical negotiations, defined as negotiation between two actors whose resources and capabilities are unequal. Traditional conceptions of power in international theory are not sufficient for understanding asymmetrical negotiation. These conceptions assume that the stronger state, by definition, will win in any encounter with a weaker state. Yet in numerous instances weaker states have won many of their objectives in negotiation with stronger states. These cases, and the inability of traditional conceptions of power to explain them, inspired this study.

Thus, a major objective of this book is the development of a framework of power that allows for a better understanding of the dynamics of the negotiation process, whether the actors be of equal or unequal power. The framework of power is tested through the analysis of three case studies of negotiation between unequal partners: the Panama Canal negotiations (1964–77), the United States–Spanish military bases negotiations (1951–76), and the Anglo-Icelandic Cod War negotiations (1958–76). The findings and conclusions derived from an analysis of these case studies assess power and tactics in weak state–strong state negotiation and may serve to guide future negotiators.

I am indebted to a number of people for their suggestions and advice during the preparation of this book. Foremost among them is I. William Zartman, whose seminar on bargaining and negotiation at the Johns Hopkins University School of Advanced International Studies first introduced me to this relatively new field. Dr. Zartman followed the development of this book from its conception to its conclusion; his questions led me to probe deeper, his suggestions invariably improved the manuscript, and his own work and innovative thinking served as an example worthy of emulation. He never ceased to encourage me.

Charles Doran, Michael Harrison, and the late Robert Osgood all read the manuscript and offered valuable suggestions and insights.

David Dessler read parts of the early drafts; my long discussions with him on power helped both to focus and expand my thinking. Former ambassadors Stephen Low and William Jorden kindly submitted to interviews that filled in many gaps in my research.

Inge Engel typed several drafts of the manuscript at her usual superhuman speed and made editorial suggestions that improved it. Jean Toll's and Melissa Vaughn's skillful editing rendered the entire manuscript clearer. Henry Tom of the Johns Hopkins University Press was extremely helpful and understanding throughout the entire process. Joni Reich offered encouragement and support from the beginning to the end and helped ensure that all of my waking hours were not spent at the typewriter. Finally, I would like to thank my employers at the Middle East Institute, and especially Philip Stoddard, who allowed me to disappear periodically during the final stages of writing.

Needless to say, none of these people has any responsibility for errors of fact or logic.

Power and Tactics in International Negotiation

ONE

Introduction: Asymmetrical Negotiation

The objective of this study is to determine, in cases of bilateral international negotiation, the effect of asymmetry between the actors on (1) each actor's ability to apply political power, (2) the choice and success of each actor's tactics, and (3) the outcome of the negotiation. The assumption is that the outcome is a function of each side's power.

Negotiation as a means of resolving disputes, managing relations, and reaching mutual decisions has become a primary activity of nation states. Although negotiation has played an important role in interstate relations for centuries, it is within the context of the nuclear stalemate of the post–World War II era that greater attention has been directed toward this particular form of decision making.[1] Most of this attention has focused on U.S.-Soviet negotiation—over arms control, economic relations, or the postwar status of Europe—or on negotiations in regions such as the Middle East, where one of the great powers often serves as mediator and where the United States and the Soviet Union have a significant stake in the outcome. In other words, most efforts to analyze international negotiation have focused on cases in which there is relative symmetry between the two actors; specifically, the symmetry in U.S.-Soviet relations brought about by the nuclear stalemate. Considerably less work has been done on asymmetrical negotiations, negotiations in which the power resources and capabilities of the two actors are unequal.

The dearth of research into asymmetrical negotiation is surprising. As Oran Young states:

> It seems reasonable to conclude on *a priori* grounds that perfectly symmetrical bargaining will seldom occur in the real world, if only because the resources and personal attributes of the players are unlikely to be identical. Situations that approximate perfectly asymmetrical bargaining, on the other hand, are probably more likely to occur in reality.[2]

Indeed, in all the negotiations in which the United States has been involved since World War II, only those with the Soviet Union have been with a relatively symmetrical opponent (even this is debatable, since only one aspect of the U.S.-Soviet relationship—the strategic/military—is characterized by relative symmetry). What accounts for the lack of research into asymmetrical negotiation?

One factor accounting for the emphasis on symmetrical negotiation is the postwar domination, until relatively recently, of the bipolar politics of the U.S.-Soviet relationship. In the 1950s and 1960s any reputable work on international relations invariably focused on this relationship. Thus, studies of negotiation also focused on U.S.-Soviet negotiations to the near exclusion of those of others. As long as the study of the international system emphasized its bipolar manifestations, other relationships were neglected.

More recently, however, emphasis on the bipolar nature of the international system has begun to wane. Stanley Hoffmann writes that bipolarity and the "security dilemma" brought about by mutual assured destruction are giving way to "asymmetrical multipolarity," characterized by new centers of power, new issues and components, and a fragmented international system.[3] In a similar vein, Edward Morse argues that "[t]he growth of regionalism in the international system . . . and the development of several types of cross-cutting interdependencies have become far more significant aspects of interstate relationships than the balance of power."[4] Thus, recognition is growing that there are important relationships other than that between the United States and the Soviet Union and that many aspects of these relationships—including negotiation—remain unexplored.[5]

Another factor that accounts for the lack of serious study of asymmetrical negotiation is the failure of mainstream international theorists to develop a framework for understanding asymmetrical relations between states. The predominant theoretical constructs of the postwar era, such as deterrence theory and theories of bipolarity, have been tailored exclusively to address problems in U.S.-Soviet relations. These theories provide an invaluable framework if one analyzes arms control negotiations, but are of little use if the analyst attempts to study trade negotiations between the United States and Latin American states, for example. Most important, the political science concept of power in international theory has no place for asymmetrical negotiation. By classical "power politics" theory, the stronger actor, that is, the actor with the greater resources and capabilities, will by definition prevail in any encounter (military or otherwise) with a weaker actor. Is it surprising, then, that classical international relations theory only finds room for studies of U.S.-Soviet negotiation? For only when there is symmetry in power, the classical argument suggests, is negotiation a phenomenon worth studying. Only when power has been "canceled out"—by being relatively equal—does negotiation become a decision-making tool of states. In all other cases—those of asymmetrical power—the stronger state, by tautological definition, will win.

Thus, a major hindrance to the analysis of asymmetrical negotiation has been the lack of a useful framework of international relations, and particularly of the concept of power in the international system. Analysts have preferred to try to force asymmetrical negotiation to "fit" into the classical framework. Thus, some analysts regard Panama's successful negotiation for sovereignty over the Panama Canal as "Jimmy Carter gave away the Panama Canal," and explain America's defeat in Vietnam as a lack of will to actualize the tremendous power disparity between the United States and North Vietnam.

But it is hardly so simple. That the weak actor often gets much of what it wants in negotiation cannot simply be ascribed to failure of will on the part of the strong. One of the objectives of this book is to show the dynamics at work in asymmetrical negotiations which account for their outcomes, dynamics that cannot easily be explained away as the classical power politicians would have us do.

A study of asymmetrical international negotiation is important not only because of the vast number of such negotiations in the contemporary world but also because it may contribute to a greater understanding of the international system as a whole. The classical approach is, and has been for a number of years, under siege. There is a growing awareness that it cannot provide a full explanation for all international events. A study that contributes to a better understanding of the limits of current theory has an importance beyond merely explaining how the weak negotiate with the strong.

Some influential works on negotiations that appeared in the decades immediately after World War II serve to illustrate the lack of attention given to asymmetrical negotiation. Fred Iklé, in *How Nations Negotiate,* hardly mentions negotiations between strong and weak states. His work, though offering many useful insights, is a product of a bipolar world.[6] Arthur Lall, in *Modern International Negotiations,* also maintains a predominantly great power focus. When he does discuss negotiations between large and small states, he almost assumes the smaller actor has no chance to achieve any of its desired outcomes. He goes so far as to argue that the more powerful actor even controls the option of whether or not to negotiate: "Power controls or contains the situation, [and] the strong country has no drastic or compelling need to discuss the issue."[7] Further on, he writes that, when there is a significant disparity of power between two sides in a negotiation, such disparity may "militate against resort to negotiation" (p. 150). If the strong country does agree to negotiate, Lall argues, its willingness to make concessions is in direct proportion to its power: "Power tends to rigidity in international negotiations, and total power tends to total rigidity" (p. 338).

Lall says that the only chance for the weak in negotiations with the strong is to adopt one of two strategies: Either form a coalition with one or the other of the great powers (i.e., join one of the bipolar blocs), or play off one of the great powers against the other, so that both will be bidding for your allegiance. Thus, according to Lall, the only power a weak state has in negotiation with a strong one is a function of another strong state's power.

The social-psychological literature on negotiation, though often presented with an aura of scientific infallibility, sheds little light on the problem of asymmetrical negotiation. Jeffrey Rubin and Bert Brown, in *The Social Psychology of Bargaining and Negotiation,* review the findings of nearly a thousand social-psychological studies, most of an experimental nature. Their research leads them to the following conclusions about power asymmetry:

> Under conditions of unequal relative power among bargainers, the party with high power tends to behave exploitatively, while the less powerful party tends to behave submissively, unless certain special conditions prevail [specifically, coalition formation by the weak].
> . . . equal power among bargainers tends to result in more effective bargaining than unequal power.
> . . . the smaller the discrepancy in bargainers' power, the more effectively they are likely to function.[8]

These findings would be eagerly supported by proponents of traditional theory. They suffer, however, from the inherent limitations of their sources, the laboratory experiments of social psychologists. The environment of the laboratory only vaguely replicates the environment of the international system. Moreover, Rubin and Brown base their conclusions on the findings of a majority of the cases they survey. Admirably democratic, but this approach does not explain what happens in those minority cases in which the high power party does not behave exploitatively, or equal power results in stalemate, or a successful outcome is reached despite a great discrepancy in power. These cases, and there are many examples in international negotiations, concern us.

A more recent work makes some notable progress. Charles Lockhart, in *Bargaining in International Conflicts,* criticizes the traditional view of power, associated with the work of Hans Morgenthau, particularly as it applies to asymmetrical negotiation. He writes: "In order to have any significant influence in bargaining, national resources must create options that are useful within the context of the specific encounters a nation faces."[9] Lockhart has made a critical break with the classical conception of power. The contextual or issue-specific nature of bargaining power will be addressed more fully in chapter 2.

Illustrating this point with an example, Lockhart refers to the U.S. defeat in Vietnam, despite the apparent preponderance of American power as classically defined. Vietnam reveals that "an asymmetry in the evaluation of stakes may offset an asymmetry in the national power of the participants in a struggle" (p. 93). In other words, power asymmetry is not, as Lall and others would have us believe, the determining factor in negotiation. Other asymmetries may be of equal importance.

In addition to nonpower asymmetries, other factors affect the negotiation outcome. Foremost is what Lockhart terms "resourcefulness," which he defines as "recognizing options usable in the conflict episode at hand" (p. 133). A similar concept will be covered in chapter 2 as part of a discussion of tactics.

Glenn Snyder and Paul Diesing, in *Conflict among Nations,* also challenge the traditional conception of power as it is applied to asymmetrical negotiations. "The military inferiority of one party may be compensated by its greater interests engaged, thus making the parties equally resolved. A militarily stronger party may be less 'resolved' in the crisis than its opponent if it does not value its interests as highly as the opponent values his."[10] Thus, like Lockhart, Snyder and Diesing stress the need to look at asymmetries beyond the traditional military/strategic one. In addition to the asymmetrical resolve mentioned in the quote is asymmetrical bargaining skill (a concept similar to Lockhart's "resourcefulness"). Snyder and Diesing recognize that bargaining skill ("virtuosity in bargaining") may lead to an outcome "somewhat different than the inherent power relations suggested" (p. 498).

What Lockhart and Snyder and Diesing do not do, however, is discuss the process of negotiation between weak and strong states. That is, though they break important ground by shedding older conceptions of power, they leave us wondering how this translates into action when strong and weak states are actually negotiating. Largely because they are not writing specifically about asymmetrical negotiation, their comments on asymmetry take the form of brief asides.

No works devoted specifically to the formulation of a theory of asymmetrical negotiation are available. Authors make passing comments about such negotiations—some, such as Lockhart's, more useful than others—but no one has yet devoted an entire study to the subject.

The rather small body of literature devoted to "small states" in international relations, though usually not specifically focused on negotiation, offers some constructive insights. Barston notes that, if a small state occupies territory of strategic importance to a larger state, it may be able to exercise bargaining influence disproportionate to its "objective" capabilities.[11] This observation suggests that the "field of play" may be as important in negotiation as the actors' respective resources and capabilities.

Bjol, building on a concept first developed by Raymond Aron, argues that a small state's ability to resist doing what a larger state wants it to do is a critical source of small state power, even if it does not have the ability to persuade the large state to do something.[12] Thus, the weaker actor's ability to hold out, or to ignore a demand made by the stronger state, may allow it to achieve its preferred outcome.

Fox, in two separate works, makes the point that small states are often able to concentrate their entire attention on the specific issue being negotiated, whereas large states must generally spread their attention over the entire international system. Fox concludes that this concentration can result in a more favorable outcome for the small actor.[13]

Finally, Vital distinguishes between "permanent and intrinsic" resources and "ephemeral and contingent" resources. The former, representing the fixed, material resources of an actor, are often less important in determining conflict outcomes than the latter, those resources relevant to the specific issue at hand.[14] This point, and the related one made by Fox, are explored more fully in chapter 2.

Some case studies of asymmetrical negotiation have, with varying success, provided useful insights. P. Terrence Hopmann set out to find the causes of asymmetrical outcomes in the bargaining at the Conference on Security and Cooperation in Europe. He observes that asymmetry refers to situations not only in which there is an imbalance in power resources but also in which "control relations" are unequal. That is, the relationship between the two actors is as important as their overall power resources. In this context, Hopmann concludes that unequal costs from failure to agree, combined with unequal capability to modify the structure of the bargaining relationship, are two determining factors of negotiation outcomes.[15]

These important findings reflect a move away from a focus on the overall power of the two actors and a look instead at the particular bilateral negotiation relationship. Moreover, by emphasizing costs of power, Hopmann encourages us to view power in net, not absolute, terms.

Yet Hopmann's analysis remains static. By failing to discuss the behavioral, dynamic aspects of negotiation, he sheds no light on *how* states negotiate under conditions of asymmetry. Nevertheless, his contribution is significant.

John Odell presents a case study of a number of bilateral trade nego-tiations between the United States and Latin American states.[16] His initial finding is that the United States won about twice as many of these negotiations as the Latin Americans. But the fact that the Latin Ameri-can states won *some* negotiations, and reached compromises in a number of others, Odell takes as evidence that the traditional view of power in negotiation needs rethinking.

He finds an explanation for the weak states' victories in "the type of strategy used by Latin American governments." He points to three strategies in particular: (1) the Latin American states often took advan-tage of the pluralist system in the United States to build domestic allies within the United States to help fight for their cause; (2) in cases in which the Latin American state possessed a commodity of particular importance to the United States, or represented a market of significant size to U.S. exporters, the threat of retaliation often resulted in an enhanced negotiation outcome; and (3) the Latin American states often came to the negotiating table with careful technical preparation and made persuasive technical arguments.

In a study of U.S.–South Korean trade negotiations, Odell reached similar conclusions. Though the United States came out ahead in the majority of the encounters, seemingly confirming the view of tradi-tional power theorists, in several "deviant" cases the South Koreans negotiated more effectively.[17]

Unlike Hopmann, Odell concentrates on the dynamics of negotia-tion between weak and strong states. He gives examples of actual strat-egies and tactics weak states have adopted in the negotiating process. He is thus one step closer to an explanation of the negotiation process, and of how behavioral aspects of power affect the negotiation's outcome.

One of the more fascinating case studies is provided by W. Howard Wriggins in his article "Up for Auction: Malta Bargains with Great Britain."[18] Wriggins gives a blow-by-blow account of Malta's negotia-tions with Britain over the future status of British bases on that island, a negotiation in which Malta greatly increased its benefits as compared to the earlier agreement. But Wriggins's work is a case study par excel-lence. His conclusions and findings are so case-specific that it is difficult to present them theoretically and apply them to other cases. His work is primarily the account of the strategy and tactics of one man, Maltese Prime Minister Dom Mintoff, and not an analysis of how weak states negotiate with strong states. Nevertheless, some tactics Mintoff used, such as making himself a "nuisance" to Britain so as to prod London into greater concessions, can be adopted in a more general theory of asymmetrical negotiation.

Another work that makes a limited though important contribution is

Peter Dobell's study of U.S.-Canadian negotiations.[19] Though it suffers from the same case-specific shortcoming as Wriggins's, it nevertheless makes the critical observation that the U.S.-Canadian *relationship,* not the overall power balance, is more important in determining the outcomes of specific U.S.-Canadian negotiations. The nature of this relationship, which is out of proportion to the relative sizes of the two states, is such that Canada is often able to negotiate successfully with its giant neighbor. This conclusion confirms Hopmann's observation, and is one of the foundations of the theoretical framework presented in chapter 2.

Robert Rothstein, in a study of the multilateral negotiations over the Integrated Program for Commodities, emphasizes the desire and need of the actors.[20] He found that the more one side wanted what was at stake, the more committed it would be and the less willing it would be to make concessions. The important role of commitment as a source of weak states' power will be addressed in chapter 2.

The most substantial case study of asymmetrical negotiation is that of I. William Zartman. In *The Politics of Trade Negotiations between Africa and the European Economic Community,* he analyzes four separate negotiations between African states and the EEC. Zartman is not bound to the traditional conception of power in asymmetrical negotiation: "The aggregate power position of a state cannot be directly translated into relevant and available power in any particular situation. Powerful states may turn out to be weak in a given confrontation with seemingly weaker states."[21] This recognition of the situational relevance of power leads to the book's key question: "How do the weak, negotiating with the strong, escape from their definitional inferiority and obtain something?" (p. ix). The very posing of this question is a breakthrough in that it acknowledges that weak states do obtain things in negotiations with strong states and directs attention to how they accomplish this.

Zartman finds three principal sources of weak states' power: (1) weak states can provoke an encounter by influencing agendas and raising points; (2) they can put forward their needs, thus pinning moral obligations on the strong; (3) weak states have the power to agree, and conversely, the power to withhold agreement.

Zartman's book is important because it addresses asymmetrical negotiation as a broader phenomenon, one that goes beyond a single case study. Moreover, by asking the right question—"*How* are convergent viewpoints combined to produce a common agreement?" (emphasis in original, p. 206)—he rightly focuses attention on the *process* of negotiation. Finally, his assumption that power is relative and situational, as opposed to aggregate and absolute, encourages further investigation

8

into exactly how power should be defined and analyzed in a negotiation framework.

The brevity of this survey indicates the dearth of material devoted to asymmetrical negotiation. The problem appears to be the concept of power, specifically, of developing an understanding of power in negotiation that allows for an analysis of cases in which the weak fare well against the strong. In another work, Zartman laments: "The important variable of power has been systematically neglected in theorizing about negotiation."[22] This neglect is indeed curious, since the negotiation process consists of the effort by two actors to reach a mutually agreeable outcome to their relationship from positions of mutual disagreement. If a mutually agreeable outcome is reached, it can only have been arrived at through the exercise of power, since it implies that one or both actors have changed their position(s) during the course of the negotiation, presumably because of the actions of the other actor.

TWO

Power and Negotiation

The concept of power has routinely been treated secondarily, if at all, in studies of negotiation. This neglect has hindered rigorous development of negotiation theory. Negotiation analysis is concerned with explaining outcomes. Explaining outcomes involves searching for causation, since negotiation outcomes are the result of a causal process. Power is "a label for a causal relation."[1] If explaining outcomes involves searching for causation, explaining causation involves seeking a notion of power. Power should thus be the principal focus of negotiation analysis. A survey of negotiation literature, however, reveals the degree to which power has been shunted to the periphery.

Many works on negotiation are, in reality, diplomatic histories of great power diplomacy. They tend to treat negotiation as the continuation of war by other means, not as a unique phenomenon of interstate interaction. As such, they see power in negotiation in the same terms as they see power in international relations as a whole. They conceive power, in the words of Inis Claude, as "essentially military capability."[2] Moreover, in this conception power is an objective as well as an effector of outcomes: "All political phenomena can be reduced to one of three basic types. A political policy seeks either to keep power, to increase power, or to demonstrate power."[3]

Negotiation theorists who adopt this conceptualization do not see power as operating any differently in negotiation than in any other aspect of international interaction, largely because they are not analyzing negotiation as a unique political phenomenon; they are studying negotiations, not negotiation.

Diplomatic accounts—those by Iklé and Lall, discussed in chapter 1, are the most prominent—thus shed little light on power in negotiation. Even those works such as Iklé's which do succeed in developing some important underlying principles of negotiation (for example, his five types of negotiation and his discussion of the "continual threefold choice") fail to deal sufficiently with the key concept of power. Whether or not they should even be considered works on negotiation theory is debatable, but not really important. What is important is that many regarded them as important works on negotiation theory, thus prolonging the idea that power in negotiation did not warrant separate study.

While these diplomatic history approaches to negotiation were failing to treat negotiation as a unique political phenomenon, the more scientific approaches to negotiation were developing too narrow and controlled a conception of negotiation. The rough heading of scientific approaches includes three broad categories: game theory, concession rate/convergence theory, and the psychological-behavioral approach. Each makes valuable contributions to negotiation theory, the most important of which is that they treat negotiation as something worthy of its own theory. Their contributions to a greater understanding of power in negotiation are spotty, however.

Game theory—exemplified in the works of Schelling, Rapoport, and Von Neumann,[4] the father of them all—reduces negotiation to rational-choice behavior. In games such as Prisoners' Dilemma and Chicken, the actors pursue a minimax strategy (minimize your losses, maximize your gains), the field of battle being a matrix of values (both theirs and the opponents'), the outcome being the intersection of the two sides' strategy choices. In game theory, the power of the two sides is derived from their respective value and reward structures, as revealed by the game matrix. But these values are assumed to be fixed and unchanging, making the outcome of many games rigidly predictable. Furthermore, most game theory presentations assume symmetry (in which case power cancels out) or have no room for the exercise of power at all.[5]

Game theory thus treats power in structural terms, specifically, the structure of the two sides' fixed values. But the process of negotiation, the process of creating outcomes, is the process of altering and modifying values. If values were truly fixed, and value structure alone determined outcomes, there would be no need to negotiate. The outcome would be predetermined. Game theory, then, describes a power structure between two sides, but not the power process.

Game theory has other deficiencies as well. Is the power structure to be determined only by weighted values? What about resources (which could be brought to bear to change values) or tactics? According to game theory, the only source of power is value and reward structures, the only tactic minimax behavior. Clearly, game theory has little relevance for the dynamic process of international negotiation, in which power has many sources and dimensions and there are at least as many possible tactics as there are actors.

The major appeal of game theory over the years has been its mathematical elegance. Moreover, game theory first rose to prominence during the rigidly bipolar cold war, in which values did appear to be fixed, tactics limited, and outcomes cataclysmic. The game of Chicken vividly depicts hypothetical nuclear crises between the United States and the Soviet Union, and the game of Prisoners' Dilemma the condition of arms control. But in the more diffuse contemporary international system, game theory is an anachronism.

Concession/convergence theories of negotiation posit that the parties start at some point of stalemate and, in an action–reaction process of responding to each other's concession rate behavior, converge toward outcome. The object of this approach is to determine why the parties make concessions at the rate they do, how the parties respond to certain concession rate behavior of the opponent, and if the parties are conceding "fairly." In short, the focus is on the rate of the parties' concessions, and how it affects the process of converging toward an outcome. Among the more notable works of the concession/convergence school of negotiation theory are those of Cross, Bartos, and Contini.[6]

Concession/convergence theories do not provide a clear conception of power. In an effort to answer the question "What makes the parties concede?" Zeuthen, Pen, and Hicks all say that the weaker party concedes more and at a faster rate.[7] In other concession/convergence theories, power enters the discussion by the back door, if at all, usually in terms of the constraints on the parties' concession behavior. For example, both Cross and Contini discuss the time costs of not conceding at a sufficiently fast rate. The party whose costs of holding out are greater generally concedes at a faster rate than his or her opponent. One can deduce therefore that the opponent would have greater power, since he or she could hold out longer.

But other connotations of power, such as power as resources, or as the tactical ability to persuade and move the other side, are not evident in the concession/convergence approaches. Like game theory, concession/convergence theories are deterministic. They assume that, once the process begins, the actors will behave in a predictable way, and that the predictable outcome determines concession rates. Some, such as Bartos, even assume that the outcome can be predicted once the bargainers' concession rates are known.[8] This deterministic quality makes it virtually impossible to inject a dynamic conception of power into concession/convergence theories, and makes them of only limited use in understanding international negotiation.

The third scientific approach to negotiation, the psychological-behavioral, is actually one of the oldest approaches. The classic works of de Callières and Nicolson are oriented toward the behavior and personality traits of the individual negotiators.[9] This orientation reappears in the more recent works of Deutsch, Rubin and Brown, and others.[10] They attempt to explain negotiation outcomes by analyzing such personality traits as "hard-line and soft-line,"[11] "interpersonal" and "motivational orientation,"[12] and "need orientation."[13] The contributions of the psychological–behavioral approach, particularly in our Freudian age, should not be underestimated. But its drawbacks are equally great. Zartman's criticism, for example, is that by "analyzing the agent rather than the process [these theories] focus on the secondary rather than the primary element of [negotiation]."[14] Moreover, they deal more with the *characteristics* of the agent than with the *actions* of the agent. It is through process and action that power and power tactics are revealed. Knowing an actor's personality traits, motivations, and needs does not explain the process by which outcomes are caused. This knowledge may, however, explain the behavior of the actors, such as responsiveness to the opponent's behavior, the choice of tactics, and so on. In this sense, it illuminates the process.

This survey of current negotiation theory reveals a void when it comes to the concept of power in negotiation. The flaw shared by all these approaches is that they are insufficient models of negotiation. They offer too narrow an understanding of a multifaceted phenomenon. Negotiation is not only strategic choice, or only concession and convergence, or only a reflection of the psychological makeup of the actors. It is all these things and more. A conception of power in negotiation must be sufficiently comprehensive if it is in any way to illuminate what happens in the causal process that leads to outcomes.

Such a conception of power must have several characteristics if it is to overcome the limitations of the approaches just reviewed. Specifically, a useful conception of power in international negotiation must

- define power independently of the negotiation's outcome. The tautological definition of power so common with the realist approach to international relations, and evident also in game theory, is in fact a nontheory. It is simply the analyst's opinion about who "won" the negotiation after the fact.
- include both the structural component of power—each actor's position at the commencement of the process—as well as the dynamic or behavioral dimension (i.e., how each actor's position changes during the course of the negotiation).
- relate to reality. That is, any useful definition of power in negotiation must be testable. It must be proven useful in analyzing real-world negotiations (and specifically, for our purposes, asymmetrical real-world negotiations).

A NEW FRAMEWORK FOR POWER IN NEGOTIATION

Political scientists have struggled for decades to come up with the ultimate and all-encompassing definition of power.[15] Many of these attempts produce theoretically rigorous definitions, but ones not always easy to break down into components or to use to explain political reality.

Power is often defined as a possession, something that actor A "has" over actor B. This way of conceptualizing power may make sense in certain contexts, such as the relationships within a society. For example, one can say that a federal regulatory agency has power over a particular industry or group, that a drill sergeant has power over his or her recruits, or that a high school principal has power over his or her students. But power within a society is allocated (in the above examples, by Congress, the army, and the school board), with the allocation process itself being the result of other power relationships. The relationships between nation-states, which are not part of a society, operate under different dynamics. Thus, it makes little sense to characterize interstate negotiation power as a possession.

Power sometimes is defined as an ability, A's ability to cause B to change his behavior. The problem with this definition is that it flirts with tautology: If A has caused a change in B's behavior, A obviously had the ability to do so. Thus, conceptualizing power as ability adds nothing to our understanding of the relationship between A and B. It is an observation, not an explanation.[16]

The fundamental problem with both of these definitions is that they view power as a static concept. It is more useful to view it as a process, which by definition is not static. Thus, power is the process by which actor A causes actor B to change his behavior. But this statement, too, is inadequate. For many things are processes; so to say that power is a process simply *classifies* power, it does not *define* it.

In order to define power, we must inquire about those characteristics and components which distinguish it from other processes. The most important component of power is resources (both aggregate and issue-specific; see below). Power is the result of having resources. But resources alone do not cause outcomes, they are merely used to create outcomes. Power thus lies between its source (resources) and its result (outcomes). It is that which creates outcomes.

Like all processes, the power process is characterized by change. Outcomes reflect the changes that have occurred during the power process, changes in the actors' positions, values, attitudes, objectives, and expectations. These changes are caused by the behavior of the other

14

actor, behavior made possible largely by the existence and use of resources.

Therefore, power is the way in which actor A uses its resources in a process with actor B so as to bring about changes that cause preferred outcomes in its relationship with B.[17] This definition should prove particularly useful in analyzing power in negotiation for several reasons.

First, it describes power as a causal process. As was noted earlier, the analysis of negotiation is the analysis of outcomes, specifically, an analysis of what causes a particular outcome instead of any other. A causal definition of power focuses attention on the process of change, and the end result of change (the outcome).

Second, this definition satisfies both those who consider power as purely intentional and those who argue that the concept must include anticipated reactions.[18] By emphasizing preferences ("preferred outcomes") the above definition allows for intentionality *and* anticipated reactions. For, as Nagel points out, "a preference is the disposition to make certain choices, not the act of choice itself."[19] To demonstrate diagramatically:

Power as Intentionality
A's preferred outcomes
↓
A's behavior
↓
B's response

Power as Anticipated Reactions
A's preferred outcomes
↓
B's anticipation of A's behavior
↓
B's response

In each instance A's preference elicits B's response. In the first instance A's behavior communicates this preference; in the second, B's perception of A's preferred outcomes elicits the response.

A definition of power in negotiation must allow for anticipated reactions. For often in negotiation an actor's demands and expectations may be determined in part by perception of the opponent's preferences, even before the opponent has evidenced any behavior that directly communicates these preferences. Opening positions, for example, are usually based in part on an evaluation of the opponent's preferred outcome and likely response. Decisions made throughout the negotiation process (on whether to be soft or firm, to threaten or concede, to walk out of the negotiations, etc.) are also greatly influenced by anticipation of the other side's reaction.

Third, this definition is relational. It focuses on one actor's ability to cause preferred outcomes in its relationship with another actor.[20] Being relational, it leaves open the possibility that B may also be achieving at least some preferred outcomes in the relationship. This aspect, too, is important for the analysis of negotiation. Negotiation implies a relationship, since there must be at least two actors to have a negotiation. Moreover, negotiation implies reciprocal power. For if only one side evidenced power in a relationship, then that side could achieve its preferred outcomes unilaterally. Unilateral achievement of outcomes is not a characteristic of negotiation; it is, in fact, the opposite of negotiation. This is not to say that each side possesses equivalent power in negotiation, or to deny that one side achieves more of its preferred outcomes than the other. Rather, it is simply saying that in negotiation—a voluntary decision-making relationship—each side can avail itself of some power, if only the power to leave the relationship.

Finally, this definition allows a structural conception of power (resources) and a behavioral conception of power (ability). Neither alone is sufficient for analyzing power in negotiation. Emphasizing resources alone does not explain the movement which is the essence of the negotiation process. Similarly, emphasizing actor skill and ability does not place the negotiation in the context of the overall relationship of the actors, and focuses on isolated moves and tactics without looking at the sources of these moves or the underlying capability to perform certain tactics. To be useful in analyzing negotiation, a definition of power must allow for both the structural and behavioral components of power.

The distinction between structural and behavioral power calls for further elucidation. The structural component describes an actor's resources, potential capabilities, and generalized position from which to actualize these capabilities. Structural power allows one to determine the relative positions of actors. To say that the United States is a great power, Britain a medium power, and Panama a small power is another way of characterizing the relative structural power positions of these three actors. Note, however, that the definition of structural power says nothing about the interaction of actors. Many analysts have used their understanding of the actors' structural positions to draw conclusions about the outcomes of their interaction: The United States will always get its way with Britain, and Britain with Panama, because of the relative structural power positions of the actors. Yet the inability of structural power to explain outcomes, as discussed earlier, has been proven empirically many times. Part of the problem lies in analysts' failure to consider the role of behavioral power (discussed in more detail below) in the determination of outcomes. A more immediate problem, however, is that most analysts talking about power mean not only structural power but generally only one subcomponent of structural power: aggregate structural power.

Aggregate Structural Power

Aggregate structural power refers to an actor's resources, capabilities, and position vis-à-vis the external world as a whole. Aggregate structural power is defined as the actor's total (or aggregate) resources and possessions. In the case of nation-states, it means total national resources—demographic, economic, and military. Ray Cline, for example, has identified the determinants of aggregate structural power as

> the size and location of territory, the nature of frontiers, the populations, the raw material resources, the economic structure, the technological development, the financial strength, the ethnic mix, the social cohesiveness, the stability of political processes and decision-making, and, finally, the intangible quantity usually described as national spirit.[21]

Aggregate structural power is not only concerned with identifying national resources. It is also concerned with national potential, the generalized ability to actualize resources. Stephen Jones describes this actualization process:

> An estimate of national power has two aspects which are related, in a figurative way, like the two rays of a triangulation. . . . One ray or beam is the conventional inventory of the elements or factors of power. It gives the power resources of a nation, using "resource" in a broad sense. The other ray is here called "national strategy."[22]

Jones then describes "national strategy" as "the art of using power for the attainment of goals in competition" (p. 422).

But Jones is talking about actualization of resources as a measure of *general* potential, the ability to organize resources efficiently, adopt a concerted international policy, and so on. He is not discussing a dynamic interaction process, discussed below as behavioral power.

Aggregate structural power is, in imagery at least, measurable. Cline has in fact concocted a "calculus of national power" for the purpose of measuring a state's aggregate structural power: $Pp = (C+E+M) \times (S+W)$; Pp = perceived power, C = critical mass (population + territory), E = economic capability, M = military capability, S = strategic purpose, and W = will to pursue national strategy.[23] In Cline's formula the elements $(S+W)$ roughly equate with Jones's concept of "national strategy."

The social exchange paradigm is based on several assumptions: (1) social behaviors have either positive or negative reinforcement values for the individual as well as for interdependent others; (2) these values are limited in availability; (3) their production implies some costs; (4) their exchange through social interaction requires allocation rules; and (5) at any given moment, someone is not satisfied, and thus will be attempting to receive more rewarding outcomes.[32] Therefore, this paradigm is a theoretical first cousin to the interdependence paradigm.

Richard Emerson was one of the first theorists to analyze the power structure of a dependent relationship in terms of social exchange theory. He equated the dependence of A on B in a relationship with the power of B over A (i.e., Dab = Pba). Thus, if Dab > Dba, then Pba > Pab. B, in this instance, would be the more powerful actor in the relationship. Emerson went on to say that one can determine the asymmetrical nature of a dependent relationship if one knows:

1. the magnitude of A's interest/desire/need for outcome x (Emerson terms this A's *motivational investment* in x),
2. the extent of control of x by B, and
3. the ability of A to find alternatives for x and/or for B.[33]

Thus, according to Emerson's paradigm, making the above three determinations for both actor A and B will reveal the power structure of the interdependent relationship. Moreover, any change in the above three characteristics of the relationship will subsequently change the relationship's power balance.

A closely related explanation of the power structure of issue-specific relationships, also based on the social exchange paradigm, is that of Thibaut and Kelley.[34] They argue that in any relationship each actor will constantly assess its comparison level for alternatives, defined as "the lowest level of outcomes a member will accept in light of available alternative opportunities" (p. 21). As long as each actor's outcomes are above its comparison level for alternatives, the relationship will continue. But more important, each actor's comparison level for alternatives "is crucial in determining his dependency upon, or conversely, his power within [the relationship]" (p. 101).

Thibaut and Kelley note that a relationship is not static and that each actor continually tries to increase its power (or decrease its dependency) by a number of means:

1. developing better alternatives to the relationship,
2. reducing the other actor's alternatives,
3. improving its ability to deliver outcomes to the other actor,

4. building up the value of its product, and
5. reducing the opponent's ability to carry out 3 and 4.

What Emerson, Thibaut and Kelley, and the interdependence theorists have in common is an emphasis on the issue-specific relationship in which the actors are involved. Their conception of power is based on the sources of power each actor derives from the relationship. Their explanation of outcomes is based on the dynamics of actor behavior within the parameters of the relationship. Moreover, they provide important insights into how to go about determining the positions of the actors in an issue-specific relationship, just as Cline provides a means of assessing the aggregate structural power balance.

Using these insights, we can say that the power balance of an issue-specific relationship is determined by three variables: alternatives, commitment, and control.

Alternatives denote each actor's ability to gain its preferred outcomes from a relationship other than that with the opposing actor. Thus, despite an aggregate power balance favoring the opponent, an actor may be able to achieve its preferred outcomes in any particular issue area if it can develop alternative relationships in which that outcome is more easily available. A weak state (in aggregate power terms) dependent upon a more powerful state for a particular natural resource may reduce that dependency, and thus the relative power of the stronger state, if it can develop a source of the needed resource from a third state.

Alternatives also explain why one actor may be able to achieve much of its preferred outcome by not negotiating, or by stalling in the negotiations. This action is related to what negotiation theorists term the "security point," the point at which the actor would prefer stalemate over negotiation. The side that has more alternatives at its security point has an advantage over the opponent.

The availability of alternatives may thus increase an actor's issue power by decreasing its dependence on the other actor. Conversely, a lack of alternatives may weaken an actor's position by increasing its dependence on the opponent. It is possible, however, that a lack of alternatives may increase an actor's motivation and therefore commitment. Iceland's economy was completely devoid of alternatives to the fishing industry, yet this condition served only to increase the Icelanders' commitment to winning the Cod Wars with Britain.

Commitment refers to the extent and degree to which an actor desires and/or needs its preferred outcome. Commitment is based on the values the parties attach to the various possible outcomes. In the Panama Canal negotiations, for example, the U.S. commitment to its preferred outcome was based on its values of commercial benefit, military uses, and prestige. Panama's commitment was based on its values of sovereignty and territorial integrity. Commitment, like alternatives, is a two-edged sword. On the one hand, greater commitment implies greater dedication to achieving preferred outcomes. Behavioral power, in this case, would be all the more directed and tenacious. On the other hand, greater desire or need for a preferred outcome would mean that the source of that outcome (the opponent, in an issue-specific relationship) would have that much more leverage in the relationship. Generally, commitment based on aspiration—a self-generated motivation—is a source of issue-power strength, whereas commitment based on need—a form of dependency—is a source of issue-power weakness. This distinction may, of course, be difficult to make in real cases. Nevertheless, it is an important one.

Control as a determinant of the issue power balance is defined as the degree to which one side can unilaterally achieve its preferred outcome despite the costs involved in doing so. In the case of negotiation, we cannot speak of total unilateral achievement of outcomes because unilateral achievement is not compatible with the concept of negotiation. But we can speak of one side's ability to gain a greater share of its preferred outcome than its opponent does. Control also is related to the "security point." For the side that receives more of its preferred outcome at its security point (i.e., unilaterally) has greater control than the opponent.

These three variables—alternatives, commitment, and control—determine the issue power balance. They are to the issue-specific relationship what material resources are to the aggregate structural relationship. Just as material resources (as defined by Cline and others) determine the aggregate structural power of an actor and the position of that actor vis-à-vis the external world as a whole, alternatives, commitment, and control establish the issue-specific structural power of an actor and its position within a relationship.

Moreover, just as the resources of aggregate structural power may compensate for one another (a large population for a technologically backward military, an advanced economy for a large population, etc.), so too alternatives, commitment, and control may compensate for one another. A lack of alternatives may be compensated for by strong commitment or greater control. A lack of control may also be compensated for by strong commitment, or by having alternatives.

Commitment, on the other hand, is a somewhat wild card. As pointed out, commitment may increase issue power if based on aspiration, but decrease issue power if based on need. A lack of commitment-as-aspiration is difficult to compensate for. If an actor has no real desire for a particular outcome, having greater alternatives or control will have little benefit. Commitment-as-need, however, may be compensated for by increasing alternatives or control, and would have the effect of reducing dependence and thus reducing need.

The issue power balance is essentially a balance of dependence. The side with greater issue power will be less dependent on the opponent for outcomes. The three components of issue power determine the issue power balance insofar as they determine each side's dependence on the other. The extent to which each side can alter its dependence depends in part upon the extent to which it can compensate for any weaknesses in its alternatives, commitment, and control.

To summarize, structural power is best analyzed at two levels: the aggregate level and the issue-specific level. At the aggregate level, the structural power balance is determined by asymmetries in national resources and capabilities. At the issue-specific level, the structural power balance is determined by asymmetries in alternatives, commitment, and control.

Structural power, however, simply describes a situation. It shows how this situation might provide one or the other actor with a power capability. But structural power alone cannot explain outcomes. Keohane and Nye write: "Power measured in terms of resources or potential may look different from power measured in terms of influence over outcomes. We must also look at the 'translation' in the political bargaining process."[35] This "translation" process is what is known as behavioral power.

Behavioral Power

As the name implies, behavioral power is concerned with the behavior of the actors: the process by which they maneuver and use their resources (both aggregate and issue-specific) to achieve preferred outcomes. In negotiation, behavioral power is revealed by the actors' tactics, which are the means by which an actor exercises power. As Christer Jönsson writes: "The exercise of power entails the conveyance of a message through some kind of signals, often a combination of verbal statements and non-verbal acts."[36]

Examples of negotiation tactics are familiar to most people: threats, warnings, promises, predictions, rewards and side payments, punishments, concessions, coalition building, stalling, and so on. Negotiation tactics are a means of communication. Specifically, they are a means of communicating preference to the other actor. But tactics are not merely used to communicate preference. They are also used to persuade and pressure the other side to fulfill these preferences. Tactics succeed by altering or modifying the issue power balance, that is, by altering each side's respective alternatives, commitment, and control within the relationship. Virtually every negotiation tactic can be seen as a means of increasing the actor's alternatives (or reducing the opponent's), increasing commitment to the actor's preferred outcome (or reducing the opponent's commitment to his or hers), or increasing the degree to which the actor can unilaterally achieve an outcome (and reducing the opponent's ability to do so).

The tactic of coalition building, for example, may increase alternatives (by forming new relationships), increase commitment (by combining several individual commitments), and increase control (by combining resources). The tactic of threats may reduce the opponent's commitment and alternatives (by communicating that the opponent's preferences and alternatives can be achieved only at greater cost than anticipated) as well as affirm the degree of control an actor possesses. Promises of rewards may reduce both the opponent's commitment to achieving his or her preferred outcome (by offering bonuses for accepting less than the preferred outcome) as well as his or her efforts to seek alternatives to the relationship. The tactic of stalling underscores one side's commitment to a preferred outcome and ability to outlast the opponent (a form of control).

Tactics thus operate at the issue-specific level. Their objective is to alter the issue-power balance, since the issue-power balance determines negotiation outcomes (or the outcomes of any other interdependent relationship). Indeed, the process of negotiation involves moving from one issue-power balance (the prenegotiation balance) to another issue-power balance (the outcome balance) by the mutual practice of tactics.

So far, tactics have been described as the policy choices of actors: one chooses to pursue a tactic of coalition building, or to assume a threatening position, or to offer rewards. But there is more to the communication process than merely choosing a particular tactic. That tactic must also be communicated at the bargaining table through the interaction of the negotiators. The opponent must be persuaded that a particular tactic is credible, that the opponent's perception of the situation needs to change, and that his or her behavior must be modified accordingly. Thus, the concept of tactics must also encompass the methods of persuasion that negotiators employ to ensure that their chosen tactical policies "work."

Persuading one's opponent of a tactic's credibility involves convincing him or her that one has the ability and will to carry out a threat, pursue alternatives, or build a coalition. Credibility is in part achieved by the existence of structural power resources (see below). But it may also involve persuasive argumentation at the negotiating table or, if this fails, more direct communication, such as walking out of the negotiations or proceeding to carry out the threatened action. An actor may possess the resources to carry out a threat, but unless he or she can also convince the other side of a willingness to do so, the threat will lack effect.

Persuasion is also used to change the opponent's perceptions. The opponent must be made to see the coalition one is forming, or the amount of control one has over outcomes, or the costs one can bring to bear on his or her efforts at control. In other words, the opponent must be persuaded to see that the issue power balance is not what he or she thinks it is. Changing the opponent's perceptions can be accomplished by argumentation but may also require less ambiguous communication, such as meeting with one's coalition partners or coercively demonstrating the extent of one's control.

The goal of persuasion is to influence the opponent's behavior: to continue doing what he or she is doing, to stop doing what he or she is doing, or to start doing something completely different. In any event, the ultimate objective in affecting behavior is to alter the issue-power balance in one's favor.

THE INTERRELATION OF THE COMPONENTS OF POWER

At first sight, aggregate structural power may seem to be out of the picture, thus suggesting the same mistake Baldwin was earlier accused of making. In fact, aggregate power resources play a major role in the communication process evidenced by tactics.

Tactics must be credible; the other side must feel that they are capable of being carried out: "The influencee will . . . look beyond the manifest message which is readily subject to manipulation, for less easily manipulated 'indices' believed to be inextricably linked to the influencer's capabilities or intentions and untainted by deception."[37] Here again, aggregate structural power can play an important role by enhancing tactics' credibility and believability. One side's tactical offer of a large financial reward or side payment in exchange for certain concessions is credible only if the offering side is perceived as possessing the needed financial resources. Similarly, a threat to use military forces is credible only if these forces exist and are deployable as threatened. Thus, the resources of aggregate structural power, translated by the tactics of behavioral power, can indirectly serve to alter the issue power balance, and thus affect outcomes. But aggregate power resources accomplish this role *only* when effectively translated by tactics.

Even while the objective of tactics is the alteration of the issue power balance, the nature of that balance may simultaneously be serving as a resource base for tactics. For example, one side's possession of greater alternatives, or lesser commitment, may allow it to follow a tactic of stalling. Thus, the credibility that ensures the success of tactics derives from aggregate power resources as well as the very issue power balance tactics are attempting to alter.

The interrelation of the components of power does not stop here. Aggregate power can partially determine the issue power balance of a relationship. Alternatives may be more readily available to an actor that enjoys great aggregate resources. Greater control may be available to the actor with the aggregate resources sufficient to maintain or achieve control. But aggregate structural power must not be seen as an absolute determinant of issue power: to do so would simply be adopting the previously discredited view of aggregate structural power. Aggregate resources alone do not determine alternatives, commitment, and control in any specific relationship. To understand to what degree they do requires the study of particular cases of issue-specific relationships.

The interaction among the components of power renders the analysis of outcomes of negotiation relationships difficult. To what degree is the nature of a particular issue-power balance independent of the aggregate power balance between the actors? Was a particular tactic a bluff, or was a credible resource backing it up? Was the change in a particular issue power balance the result of a credible tactic, or of the realization of an aggregate power disparity between the actors? Which component of power was most important in determining the outcome?

Answers to questions such as these can be found only in the case studies of actual negotiations. Since the assumption (discussed in chapter 1) is that aggregate structural power alone does not determine negotiation outcomes, the most useful cases to study are those with an aggregate structural power disparity between the actors, in other words, cases of asymmetrical negotiation. For only these cases can shed light on the roles of the issue power balance and of tactics (behavioral power).

THREE

The Negotiation Process

Developing a framework for the concept of power in negotiation requires a framework of process. For if each negotiation were characterized by a unique process, then the role of power could be analyzed only case by case; it would be difficult to reach any enduring theoretical conclusions. A framework of process will enable us to reach general conclusions from studying a limited number of cases.

The search for a framework of process is not new. The results of such searches, however, have been remarkably similar. Most analysts end by defining the negotiation process as a series of offers, demands, and concessions, in which the two sides inch toward an agreement. This conception of the negotiation process has an intuitive appeal, since it reflects the average person's perception of what happens in negotiation.

A selective review of negotiation literature reveals the universal popularity of the offer-counteroffer view of process. Iklé describes the negotiation process as one in which each side offers proposals, makes arguments to support those proposals, and then makes concessions until a compromise agreement is reached.[1] Rubin and Brown define the negotiation process as a sequential one, one that "involves the presentation of demands or proposals by one party, evaluation of these by the other, followed by concessions and counterproposals."[2] A recent popular work on negotiation, Howard Raiffa's *The Art and Science of Negotiation,* presents a similar process. Each side makes offers, gauges the other side's reaction to these offers, and then makes concessions until agreement is reached. "The most common pattern of concessions is monotone decreasing—that is, the intervals between . . . decreasing offers becomes successively smaller."[3]

The view of the negotiation process as one of offer-counteroffer has been developed by the concession/convergence school of analysis, which focuses on how each party reacts to the other's concession behavior. Otomar Bartos, for example, posits that negotiators view the midpoint between their past demands and offers as a just solution and work

27

to achieve this midpoint. The negotiation process thus consists of each side assessing, and revising if necessary, its expectations about what the ultimate agreement will be, based on the concession behavior of the opponent.[4] Similarly, John Cross sees the negotiation process as one of adapting expectations: "Negotiators . . . choose bargaining strategies in their attempt to optimize their payoffs from the situation. These strategies are contingent on each party's perception of the strategy of his opponent [i.e., of his opponent's demands and concession rates]."[5] Cross concludes that a party will concede in reverse proportion to the opponent's concession rate.

Concession/convergence approaches to the negotiation process have an intuitive attraction since all negotiations involve concessions and all successful negotiations involve convergence. But unfortunately these approaches, and the offer-counteroffer approaches, leave many questions unanswered. How, for example, do negotiations start? What prompts each side to believe that a move away from stalemate will result in a desired outcome? Once the decision to negotiate has been made, how do the parties determine what issues are to be negotiated and what the limits or boundaries of the negotiation are to be? Only after such questions have been answered can we begin to look at each side's rate of concession and at the dynamics of mutual convergence.

Zartman detects another problem: Concession/convergence does not always reflect the negotiation process in real-world cases. His assertion is based on a survey-research study in which diplomats with negotiation experience were questioned about their perception of the negotiation process and asked to take part in a number of mini-scenarios.[6] Zartman's findings led him to challenge the offer-counteroffer conception of the negotiation process with a new framework, "formula-detail":

> Rather than a matter of convergence through incremental concessions from specific initial positions, negotiation is a matter of finding the proper *formula* and implementing *detail*. Above all, negotiators seek a general definition of the items under discussion, conceived and grouped in such a way as to be susceptible of joint agreement under a common notion of justice. Once agreement on a formula is achieved, it is possible to turn to the specifics of items and to exchange proposals, concessions and agreements.[7]

The formula-detail approach, as developed by Zartman and Berman in *The Practical Negotiator*, presents negotiation as a three-stage process: the diagnostic phase, the formula phase, and the detail phase.

THE FORMULA-DETAIL APPROACH

The Diagnostic Phase

At some point each side recognizes that a negotiated solution to their conflict is possible. The prenegotiation activity leading to this realization is termed the diagnostic phase. It is the phase in which each side explores the costs and benefits of a negotiated solution. For example, each side may realize that neither actor can achieve its objectives unilaterally, or that new solutions need to be invented for new problems and conflicts. In either of these instances, the decision to negotiate would be a logical conclusion.

The actors may also recognize that changes have occurred in the nature of their relationship. The actors may perceive that relative power positions have changed: "The former upper hand slips, or the former underdog improves his position."[8] Similarly, a perceived or real change in the structure and nature of the actors' system may have occurred, leading to a questioning of old norms, or to the introduction of new issues and actors; either may convince the parties that new solutions are in order.

In general, two characteristics must be present for the diagnostic phase to end with a decision to begin negotiating: "The parties agree that they need a solution and that their decision on a solution must be unanimous" (p. 46). This decision is reached before formal interaction between the actors; negotiation, as such, has not begun. Rather, in the diagnostic phase each actor is assessing the possibility that negotiation is in order. Though this assessment may be strongly affected by the course of events, it is essentially an internal decision-making process. The key factor, according to Zartman and Berman, is will: "Without the will to reach an agreement, there will be none" (p. 66).

At some point during the diagnostic phase, a "turning point of seriousness" will be reached when "each side [perceives] that the other is serious about finding a negotiated solution—that is, that the other is willing to 'lose' a little to 'win' a little rather than win or lose all in a non-negotiated approach" (p. 87). This turning point is not necessarily perceived by both sides at the same time, nor need it be formally communicated. Moreover, the turning point of seriousness may need to be renewed several times throughout the negotiations. The Panama Canal negotiations, for example, witnessed three such turning points: President Johnson's decision to negotiate in 1964, the Kissinger-Tack principles of 1973, and again in the spring of 1977, several months before an agreement was finally reached.

The Search for a Formula

After the parties have jointly determined that negotiation is both possible and desirable, they enter the formula phase of the negotiation. This phase is characterized by a search for general principles, or formula. Zartman and Berman define formula as "a shared perception or definition of the conflict that establishes terms of trade, the cognitive structure of referents for a solution, or an applicable criterion of justice" (p. 95).

A shared perception of the problem is probably the single most important element of a formula, for without it the two sides would remain hopelessly stalemated. A solution to the Anglo-Icelandic Cod Wars was so difficult to reach largely because Iceland perceived the problem as overfishing, whereas Britain insisted that the problem was the illegality of unilaterally extending territorial waters.

Referents relate to "the secondary or underlying values that give meaning to the items under discussion" (p. 98). The development of joint referents was a critical aspect of the U.S.–Spanish bases negotiations. In the first negotiations in 1951–53, as well as throughout the three ensuing negotiations, the United States and Spain were constantly trying to put together packages of referents centered on base rights, economic aid, and mutual defense arrangements.

The third characteristic of formulas—the establishment of a criterion of justice—is often the key element in tying the formula together. In the Panama Canal negotiations, the United States initially held an equitable conception of justice. That is, the outcome should be apportioned on the basis of each party's investment in the Canal. Since the United States had constructed the Canal and defended it for over sixty years, the United States deserved special benefits and rights from a new treaty. Panama, on the other hand, held a compensatory conception of justice. Those who are in greater need, or who have been treated unfairly in the past, should receive favorable treatment. It was not until the two sides had developed a conception of justice somewhere in between these two extremes that a formula, and thus a solution, became possible.

In the formula phase, the parties generally are in direct contact with each other; actual negotiation has begun. But this phase is not characterized by the horse-trading associated with offer-counteroffer conceptions of negotiations. Instead of demanding and conceding points, the parties are attempting to define points: What exactly is to be negotiated? What are the boundaries of a fair and just solution? What are the underlying principles and shared values that will guide each side's demands and concessions?

The outcome of this phase is the acceptance by both parties of a mutually agreeable formula. Although the formula is often embodied in a distinct, formal agreement or document (as in the Panama Canal negotiations), such formalization need not be the case. Often, the formula can only be detected in hindsight, and the parties themselves may not even realize they have found one. Nevertheless, the survey conducted by Zartman and Berman reveals that in most cases the parties found a formula and used it to guide the ensuing bargaining over details.

The Detail Phase

"The detail phase consists of a long, tense search for agreement on details to implement the general framework set out in the previous [i.e., formula] phase" (p. 199). It is the phase that most resembles the offer-counteroffer conception of the negotiation process. In the detail phase, the parties send signals (offers and demands), make concessions, exchange points (converge), arrange details, and finally bring the negotiation to an end. Because the detail phase consists of what most people associate with negotiation, it is often assumed to represent the entire negotiation process. Indeed, this is the mistake of the offer-counteroffer theorists.

ZARTMAN and Berman preempt much criticism by pointing out that their various phases, as conceptualized, are considerably neater and more distinct than they are in reality. The diagnostic phase, for example, may go on throughout the entire course of the negotiations; as contextual events change, the parties may have to renew continually their commitment to negotiation. The parties may also begin negotiating details before, or simultaneous with, reaching a clearly defined formula. Moreover, the formula itself may be subject to refinement throughout the negotiation process. Even the diagnostic phase is subject to some flexibility. The parties may begin creating a formula before reaching a firm conclusion that negotiation is really possible.

But formula-detail is meant merely as a framework for better understanding what is in reality a complex and fluid process. And for this purpose, it is considerably more useful than the offer-counteroffer theories. It provides a guide to what happens from the very beginning of the process (the prenegotiation, or diagnostic, phase), and offers a basis for answering those questions raised earlier: How do negotiations start? What prompts each side to move away from stalemate? How do the parties determine what issues are to be negotiated and the boundaries of the negotiation?

TURNING POINTS

Progression from one phase of the negotiation process to another is not automatic. It generally requires a breakthrough or, in Druckman's terminology, a "turning point."[9] As we saw above, the diagnostic phase often culminates in a "turning point of seriousness," a perception by the two sides that a negotiated solution to their conflict is realistic and desirable. Similarly, the mutual acceptance of a formula is the turning point that moves the negotiations into the detail phase.

Druckman distinguishes two types of turning points: those that occur after an impasse or stalemate (a period of no progress), and those that occur after a crisis (a threat to the continuation of the negotiations). In the former case, the turning point is more likely to lead to progression to a new phase in the process. In the latter case, the turning point salvages the negotiations but does not necessarily move them forward (p. 8). "The speed with which a negotiation progresses . . . depends largely on the incidence of turning points relative to crises" (p. 6).

Druckman's contribution to the formula-detail conception of the negotiation process alerts us to key moments in negotiations, moments that signal progression from one phase to another. He helps us focus on those critical junctures on which the fate of the negotiations may hinge.

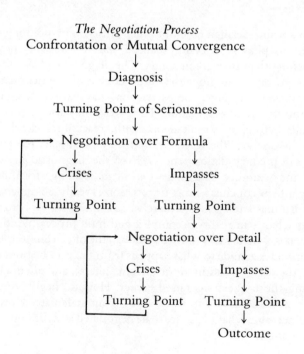

The Negotiation Process
Confrontation or Mutual Convergence
↓
Diagnosis
↓
Turning Point of Seriousness
↓
Negotiation over Formula
↓   ↓
Crises   Impasses
↓   ↓
Turning Point   Turning Point
↓
Negotiation over Detail
↓   ↓
Crises   Impasses
↓   ↓
Turning Point   Turning Point
↓
Outcome

On the practical level, greater understanding of Druckman's concepts may help guide people to negotiate better: "Anything that negotiators can do to increase the size of this 'ratio' [between turning points and crises] should move the talks along" (p. 6).

FOUR

The Panama Canal Negotiations

The negotiations between the United States and the Republic of Panama over the status of the Panama Canal provide a classic example of asymmetrical negotiation. Not only was the United States superior to Panama in aggregate structural power, there was moreover a long history of unilateral American actions in Panama and the rest of Central America. The very founding of the Republic of Panama was in large measure the result of unilateral U.S. actions directed against Colombia, of which Panama was a part before 1903. The original Panama Canal Treaty of 1903, although formally signed by a representative of the Panamanian government, was in fact a nonnegotiated document drawn up to meet virtually all of the demands of the American government.[1] In sum, before 1964, there was little historical precedent for the United States to negotiate an important political agreement with a Central American state; unilateralism was the norm.

The riots of January 1964 served as a catalyst for the first true negotiations between the two countries. Panama had expressed strong dissatisfaction with the 1903 treaty as early as 1904. The United States responded to Panama's complaints by offering Panama some minor concessions, but linked them to additional obligations on the part of the Panamanians, who rejected the package. In 1935, under President Roosevelt's Good Neighbor policy, the United States agreed to the Hull-Alfaro Treaty, which limited the American right to intervene in Panamanian domestic affairs (a right guaranteed by the 1903 treaty) and raised the annual U.S. payment to Panama for use of the Canal Zone. In 1955, another agreement once again raised U.S. payments. But neither of these agreements was the result of true negotiations. The Hull-Alfaro Treaty was motivated by the broader U.S. strategic objective of ensuring Latin American friendship in the event of war with Nazi Germany; the 1955 agreement was an attempt to appease Panama during the early, tense years of the Cold War. Neither was the result of the give and take of real negotiation.

Moreover, these agreements failed to address the longstanding Panamanian desire to abrogate the 1903 treaty with its hated "in perpetuity" clause. This clause gave the United States perpetual control of the Canal Zone "as if it were sovereign."[2] Even while making cosmetic concessions, the United States for years had refused to consider renegotiating the 1903 treaty. Following the tumultuous events of 1964 the United States finally agreed to discuss a new treaty that would give Panama sovereignty over the Canal, the issue over which Panama had wished to negotiate for most of the twentieth century.

This analysis will end with the treaties signed in Washington on September 7, 1977. It will not deal with U.S.-Panamanian relations between that date and June 16, 1978, when the formal instruments of ratification were signed in Panama City, even though several major political confrontations occurred during that period. These confrontations were primarily related to the intragovernmental negotiations in the United States between the executive and legislative branches over Senate ratification of the treaty, and are not considered here as part of the bilateral international negotiation.[3]

THE PRECRISIS ISSUE POWER BALANCE

At the beginning of 1964, the United States possessed an extreme issue power advantage in its relationship with Panama. As discussed in chapter 2, the issue power balance describes the nature of the interdependency between two actors, a function of the two sides' respective alternatives, commitment, and control.

Alternatives

Alternatives denote each actor's ability to gain its desired outcome from a relationship other than that with the opposing actor. In the years before 1964, the United States possessed the ability (based on its tremendous structural power resources, and specifically, its financial resources) to construct a new canal elsewhere in Central America. Whether this was truly a viable alternative is debatable (it was in fact eventually determined not to be viable, see below). But the existence of this ability on paper provided the United States with an alternative to its relationship with Panama.

Panama, on the other hand, had no alternatives for achieving its desired outcome (sovereignty over the Canal) in a relationship outside of that with the United States. There was only one canal in Panama and this canal was under American control. Thus, Panama's desired outcome could only be achieved through its relationship with the United States.

Furthermore, Panama's economic well-being was largely dependent upon the U.S. presence in the country, U.S. payments for use of the Canal Zone (meager as they were), and U.S. economic interests in the country. Thousands of Panamanians worked in the Canal Zone, and thousands more sold their produce and manufactures through the Zone. The United States was Panama's primary trading partner and chief source of capital. Conversely, Panama was but one relatively insignificant trading partner of the United States.

To summarize, the United States held a clear advantage over Panama in terms of alternatives. This aspect of the two actors' interdependency was severely unbalanced.

Commitment

Commitment has been defined as the degree to which an actor desires and/or needs its preferred outcome. Commitment is a function of an actor's value structure: the more an actor values an outcome, the more committed it will be to achieving that outcome. Before 1964, the American commitment to maintaining control of the Panama Canal was considerable. The United States viewed the Canal as a major and significant strategic asset, particularly in the period before the U.S. Navy had become a two-ocean fleet. The navy's one-ocean fleet greatly depended on the Canal, since it substantially shortened the time required to move portions of the fleet from the Atlantic to the Pacific. However, after the advent of the two-ocean fleet, the U.S. need for the Canal as a strategic asset diminished. Moreover, the development of intercontinental ballistic missiles in the late 1950s rendered the Canal vulnerable to instantaneous destruction, thus significantly devaluing it as a strategic asset.

But the United States had additional sources of its commitment to maintaining control of the Canal. Thousands of Americans and their families lived in the Canal Zone, representing a well-organized and influential bloc with a number of powerful allies in Congress. In addition, the majority of the American public genuinely believed the Canal Zone to be a part of the United States. The miraculous feat of constructing the Canal was part of American folklore; as perhaps the preeminent symbol of American ingenuity, the Canal inspired a strong commitment to maintaining sovereignty.

Despite the strong American commitment to its desired outcome, the Panamanians had an even greater commitment. No other single issue aroused Panamanians as did the Canal. The Panamanians had lodged their first official complaint about the 1903 treaty in 1904.[4] Thereafter, the Canal question loomed as the most important issue in Panamanian elections and among intellectuals, students, and the press. An unwavering commitment to the goal of achieving sovereignty over the Canal was a prerequisite for any Panamanian wishing to advance politically. The issue transcended all levels of society, and in many ways served as a unifying cause for the entire nation.

Control

Control as a determinant of issue power has been defined as the degree to which each side can unilaterally achieve its preferred outcome. Before 1964, the United States clearly possessed the advantage of control. In the years after the completion of construction of the Canal in 1914, the United States established a number of military bases in the Canal Zone, and stationed up to 12,000 U.S. military personnel in the Zone at any given time.[5] The purpose of this military presence was to guarantee continued American control of the waterway. A number of American military interventions in Central America in the early 1900s provided clear evidence that the United States was indeed willing to use military force to secure its perceived interests. These included military actions in Nicaragua in 1910 and 1912, in Cuba in 1912, in Haiti in 1916, and several interventions in Panama itself during periods of domestic instability.[6]

In contrast to the American military presence in Panama, the Panamanians themselves were in a greatly inferior position. Panama had no armed forces beyond its small, 4,000-strong National Guard, whose function was that of a national police force. Faced with American military preponderance, and evidence of American willingness to use its military power to protect its interests, the National Guard stood little or no chance of achieving Panama's preferred outcome of sovereignty over the Canal. Until 1936, the United States enjoyed the legal right to intervene in Panamanian domestic politics. Even after President Roosevelt agreed to surrender this right, there was little doubt the United States would still exercise it if deemed necessary to protect the Canal.

Between 1914 and 1964 Panamanians directed several incidents of public protest against American control of the Canal. The most serious were the 1959 riots, which led the Eisenhower administration to agree to fly both the American and Panamanian flags at one location in the Zone, near the entrance to Panama City. None of these incidents, however, seriously threatened to lead to the achievement of Panama's desired outcome, largely because of the U.S. military presence. They were, however, evidence of the degree of Panamanian commitment to the goal of winning sovereignty over the Canal.

Thus, before 1964, the United States enjoyed a favorable issue power balance. The United States possessed alternatives to its relationship with Panama, a strong commitment to the goal of retaining the 1903 treaty, and, most important, virtual unilateral control over outcomes. Panama, while expressing an intense commitment to gaining sovereignty over the Canal, had neither alternatives to its relationship with the United States nor the ability to achieve unilaterally its desired outcome.

This issue power imbalance explains why renegotiating the 1903 treaty was never seriously attempted before 1964. Although the United States also enjoyed a tremendous structural power advantage, and although this structural power advantage was partially responsible for the American issue power advantage, it is on the issue power balance that the prospects for negotiation depend. Thus, even though Panama continued to suffer from a structural power disadvantage, its efforts to alter the issue power balance in the period after 1964 proved decisive in bringing about negotiations for a new treaty.

THE CRISIS

In June 1962, Panamanian President Roberto Chiari visited President Kennedy in Washington to discuss overall relations between the two countries. Much of the discussion was devoted to questions of U.S. economic aid and the threat Fidel Castro's Cuba posed to Central America. But Chiari also brought up the Canal issue. For several years, signs of unrest among Panamanian students had been growing.[7] This unrest was caused primarily by economic frustrations, such as unemployment, yet it had begun to take on an anti-American theme. Chiari hoped his talks with Kennedy would result in at least some symbolic American actions to help defuse Panama's domestic tensions.

Kennedy obliged by agreeing to establish a joint commission to study outstanding issues between the two countries. The commission's mandate was vague; it was by no means charged with discussing the status of the Canal. Yet one of its cosmetic concessions to Panama was the decision to allow the Panamanian flag to fly alongside the American flag at a select number of civilian institutions in the Canal Zone.[8]

The American citizens who lived in the Canal Zone were infuriated by this concession to the Panamanians. They had long regarded the Canal Zone as United States territory, though the 1903 treaty did not consider it to be.[9] Zonian anger grew steadily over the next year. In early January 1964, a group of "radical" Zonians decided that only the

American flag would fly at the Zone's Balboa High School, one of the institutions designated by the commission for the flying of both flags. On January 9, several hundred Panamanian students, aware of the Zonians' action, marched into the Zone to raise their flag at the school. Several hundred American students were at the flagpole to greet them. The few dozen Canal Zone policemen could do nothing to prevent the inevitable confrontation. Thus began the riots of 1964.

Word spread quickly. Within several hours tens of thousands of protesters were in the streets of Panama City, marching toward the Zone and looting stores and shops along the way. By evening, it was clear that U.S. troops would be needed to protect the entrances to the Zone. The ensuing events have been recounted in detail elsewhere.[10] It is sufficient to note here that over the next several days more than twenty people were killed, including three American soldiers, and several hundred were injured.[11]

The immediate cause of the January riots was the confrontation at the Balboa High School flagpole. But the underlying cause and the reason the protest spread so rapidly and so completely throughout Panama was the decades of frustration Panamanians had felt over their lack of control over the Canal. Aware of the historical roots of the crisis, President Chiari was quick to transform it into a catalyst for bringing about negotiations for a new Canal treaty.

This action represented a tactic of crisis exploitation. Chiari used the crisis, and the threat he knew it posed to the United States, to try to focus attention on Panama's longstanding desire to renegotiate the 1903 treaty. The first step in this tactic was to refuse to call out the Panamanian National Guard to put down the crisis. In past anti-American demonstrations in Panama the National Guard had generally helped to ensure that the protesters did not get out of hand. But Chiari chose to allow the rioters to control events—and headlines. There was to be no doubt on the part of Americans that Panamanians were angered by the continuing U.S. presence in their country.

Chiari's second step was to break diplomatic relations with the United States. In a telephone conversation with President Johnson, the Panamanian leader said that the riots were caused by the frustrations of the Panamanian people over the U.S. presence, that there had to be a "complete revision" in the 1903 treaty, and that Panama would not resume formal ties until the United States agreed to renegotiate the Canal treaty.[12]

The third step in Chiari's crisis exploitation tactic was to internationalize the Canal issue. Panama called an emergency meeting of the Organization of American States (OAS) on January 9, when, for the first time in the history of that organization, the United States was accused of aggression. Chiari also called for an emergency meeting of the United Nations Security Council.

Chiari hoped that the riots, combined with his breaking of diplomatic relations and internationalization of the issue, would be sufficient prodding to bring the United States to the negotiating table.

More specifically, he was attempting to alter the issue power balance. Allowing the riots to run their violent course communicated two things: First, it demonstrated the extent of Panama's commitment to a new treaty. After the riots, the United States could no longer delude itself into thinking that only a small, radical minority of Panamanians desired a revision in the 1903 agreement, and that minor reforms would pacify Panama. Second, the January riots raised serious questions about control; could the United States continue to maintain the security of the Canal against an aroused Panamanian public?

The Diagnostic Phase

Although the Panamanians succeeded in communicating their frustrations, President Johnson, shocked by this major crisis so early in his presidency, refused to agree to Chiari's terms. He indicated that the United States was willing to discuss any grievances, but only "within the context of the [1903] treaties."[13] But Johnson would not negotiate under pressure; only after relations between the two countries were normalized would the Americans agree to discuss grievances.

A two-month-long stalemate followed, despite attempts at mediation by the OAS. Panama quickly began to feel the effects of its decision to break relations with the United States. Private American investment in Panama nearly ground to a halt. Other foreign business interests also grew wary of the situation in the country. By late January, Chiari was under pressure from the Panamanian business community to end the stalemate.[14] The prospect of a long-term chill in U.S.-Panamanian relations had terrifying implications for an economy so dependent upon its giant neighbor. Not willing to give in so quickly, Chiari tried to find alternative sources of financial support. With the country's foreign reserves dwindling, he dispatched a group of leading Panamanian business and political figures to several world capitals in search of economic support. They met with success only in Madrid, where the Franco government agreed to provide Panama with an interest-free loan of $5 million.[15] This gave Chiari a little breathing room to sustain his standoff with the United States.

But the situation worsened throughout February. The OAS abandoned its unsuccessful efforts at mediation. There was no change in Johnson's refusal to negotiate prior to reestablishment of normal relations. And in Panama economic confidence continued to deteriorate despite the Spanish loan. It appeared that Chiari's tactic of transforming the January 4 riots into new treaty negotiations was failing.

Throughout this period President Johnson tried to find a compromise, though one that would appear not to be giving in to Chiari's tactics. In late January, Johnson announced that the United States would enter into negotiations with Panama "without preconditions."[16] This announcement seemed to leave the door open to discussing the status of the Canal. Several days later the United States agreed to specific mentioning of the Canal as one of the issues to be reviewed in talks between the two countries.[17] In early March, Johnson said that "adjustments" might be required in the Canal treaty, but he reiterated that there could be no talks until relations were normalized.[18] This conceding language by the United States was designed to give Chiari an excuse to resume ties and commence talks. The Americans were well aware of the economic burden on Panama caused by Chiari's tactic and were attempting to lure him to the negotiating table. But the United States was also making it clear that, despite the concessions, there would be no agreement beforehand to renegotiate the 1903 treaty.

Finally, in late March, the United States made its last concession. At an impromptu White House press conference, Johnson said he would be willing to "view every issue that now divides us, and every problem which the Panamanian Government wishes to raise."[19] This statement was essentially a rewording of the two earlier ones, an indication that Johnson would go no further. With the Panamanian economy deteriorating, time was on the Americans' side.

Another factor was on the Americans' side. In February, the Department of Defense had sent a report to President Johnson urging him to consider building a new canal across Central America. A new canal would be built at sea level, thus obviating the need for locks. It would reduce the need for foreign personnel, and make sabotage more difficult, since canal locks were ideal targets for saboteurs. A new canal would also be larger than the Panama Canal, open to the many large ships that could not traverse the existing waterway.

When news of this report reached Panama, it sent chills through the country's leadership, for the Canal is to Panama what oil is to Saudi Arabia. The sobering thought that the United States might be pushed into abandoning it for a new canal in a neighboring country was the final blow to Chiari's tactic. The United States was employing the threat to pursue alternatives, alternatives disastrous to Panama, as a means of breaking Panamanian resolve. This threat was effectively combined with Johnson's conceding statements, putting domestic pressure on Chiari to end the stalemate.

On April 3, Panama and the United States agreed to a joint communiqué calling for resumption of diplomatic relations and "the prompt elimination of the causes of conflict between the two countries."[20] This was a far cry from Panama's initial demand that the United States agree to renegotiate the 1903 treaty. But several sources indicated that the United States had privately assured Panama that all Panamanian concerns would be treated in good faith.[21] Moreover, in another concession to Panama, the final point of the joint declaration stated that the objective of the upcoming consultations would be "a just and fair agreement which would be subject to *the constitutional process of each country*."[22] It seemed to suggest a possible new treaty.

At the end of the 1964 riots, and the ensuing stalemate, the issue power balance had been slightly altered in Panama's favor. The Panamanians had demonstrated their great commitment to gaining control of the Canal. The degree of this commitment, and the passion with which it was held, had often gone unnoticed by Americans. The 1964 riots awakened the U.S. government to the intensity of Panama's grievances. President Johnson later admitted that the riots convinced him that "it was indeed time to take a fresh look at our treaties."[23]

Panama also gained in the control component of issue power. This is not to say that Panama demonstrated an ability to achieve unilaterally its preferred outcome (i.e., to capture the Canal by force). But it had demonstrated an ability to disrupt, and thus to threaten and make more costly, America's continued control over the Canal. The distinction is between the ability to achieve one's objectives and the ability to prevent the opponent from achieving his objectives. The 1964 riots were the most violent anti-American demonstrations ever in Panama. The Americans were forced to call out armed forces, who suffered a number of casualties, all in a brief period. The prospect of a more prolonged Panamanian assault on the Canal must have now been viewed with considerable trepidation in Washington. In short, the United States was forced to reassess "the probability that the status quo in Panama could be maintained without unacceptable costs."[24]

Panama was not successful, however, in its search for alternatives to its relationship with the United States. The economic crisis caused by the break in relations with the United States was disastrous to Panama's small economy. Its inability to find alternative sources of financial support, other than the small loan from Spain, only underscored Panama's lack of alternatives to the United States.

As for the United States, the crisis revealed a continued, if now weakened, predominance in the control component of issue power. Panama was not, at least for the time being, capable of taking the Canal Zone by force. But more important, the United States demonstrated its tremendous predominance in the alternatives component of issue power. The leaked threat to build a new canal was the ultimate American card. It reminded Panama that the United States was capable of, and willing to consider, achieving its preferred outcome outside of its relationship with Panama. This ability was a function of American structural power, specifically, the financial and technological resources necessary to undertake construction of a new canal.

By April 1964, the two sides had learned a great deal about each other's capabilities and desires. Although the Panamanians' tactic of fueling and exploiting the crisis had backfired, leading as it did to near economic collapse, it had also shocked the United States into acknowledging that negotiations between the two countries were unavoidable. The United States, by threatening to build a new canal outside of Panama, had successfully demonstrated that the issue power balance would have to be altered to a substantially greater degree before Panama could hope to achieve its most desired outcome.

The Search for a Formula, Part 1

The bilateral talks called for in the April 3 agreement commenced in July. At the first negotiating session, the two sides began the search for a formula by restating their desired outcomes. Panama said the agenda of the talks should emphasize recognition of Panamanian sovereignty over the Canal, increased economic benefits for Panama, Panamanian participation in Canal administration, and, most important, a fixed date on which the 1903 treaty would terminate. The United States insisted that the talks emphasize a continued U.S. role in running the Canal, means of assuring defense of the Canal, and continued U.S. legal jurisdiction over American citizens in the Canal Zone.[25] Neither side accepted the other's proposed agenda, but each appeared willing to continue the search for a formula.

The primary U.S. tactic over the next several months was to continue developing its alternatives. Just two weeks after the April 3 agreement, the United States and Colombia announced an accord to begin a feasibility study of a sea-level canal through Colombia. Washington also announced that it would explore the possibility of building a new canal through Nicaragua or southern Mexico. Johnson administration sources told the New York Times that Panama was not being considered for a new canal "because of the recent diplomatic and political difficulties."[26] These statements should have rid the Panamanians of any doubts that the United States was prepared to exploit fully its issue power advantage.

At the opening session of the talks the United States reiterated this option. After each side had presented its proposed agenda, the American negotiators briefed their Panamanian counterparts on the need for a new canal and on America's ability to build one. In the words of William Jorden: "The briefing was a not so subtle reminder to the Panamanians that the United States was seriously thinking of replacing the old canal. . . . A chill settled over the Panamanian delegation when they considered that the canal . . . might within a few years become no more than a tourist attraction."[27]

The U.S. tactic of emphasizing its alternatives, and thus reducing its dependence on Panama and increasing its issue power position, resulted in a slowing of the negotiation process. The Panamanians felt it would be difficult to proceed more rapidly until the United States made a decision on a new canal.[28] But they continued to insist that their objective remained a new canal treaty and eventual Panamanian control of the Canal Zone.

After several months of stalemate, the Johnson administration altered its tactic. Robert Anderson, the chief American negotiator, became convinced that the Panamanians were not going to back down from their demand for a new treaty. He suggested that the United States offer a new proposal that would agree to a fixed termination date for the old treaty but would also give the United States the right to dig a new canal in Panama. Furthermore, the United States would retain the right to defend both the old and the new canal, even after termination of the 1903 treaty.[29]

President Johnson agreed to this proposal. On December 18, 1964, he announced that the United States would negotiate a new treaty with Panama and would simultaneously proceed with plans to build a new canal.[30] He did not, however, say where the new canal would be located, naming northern Colombia and the Costa Rican–Nicaraguan border, as well as Panama, as possible sites. Moreover, it would take four years to complete the study to determine the best location for a new canal. Johnson thus implicitly linked the negotiations for a new treaty with the question of a new canal.

Initially, the Panamanians reacted favorably to the new American proposal. Nearly a year after the turbulent riots, the United States had finally acknowledged that a new treaty must be negotiated to replace the inequitable 1903 treaty. As such, the Panamanians perceived this announcement as a "turning point of seriousness,"[31] a stated willingness by the Americans to compromise for the sake of a solution. But on closer analysis it was evident that the new American proposal was double-edged. For while it acknowledged the need for a new treaty, it maintained the American alternative of constructing a new canal in Central America. This alternative meant that the Panamanians would be negotiating in the dark, since they had no assurances the new canal would be built in Panama. By thus flaunting its potential alternatives, the United States greatly increased its issue power position. Panamanian uncertainties about whether the United States would choose its alternative made it difficult for Panama to push its demands. Surveying the situation, one Panamanian official remarked: "The United States is playing a giant's game of poker. The stakes are so big nobody can afford to make a mistake."[32]

Anything that might encourage or promote the sort of anti-American sentiment that led to the 1964 riots would have been a mistake for Panama. Not only would this approach risk more economic chaos, it could push the United States into building a new canal elsewhere. Thus, the Panamanian government had to moderate its tone when discussing its demands. This necessity greatly weakened what had been Panama's most effective tactic, the tacit threat of disruption or violence.

But the Panamanians did not have to give in to the U.S. position. They knew that constructing a new canal, though certainly a possibility given American structural power, would be a massive undertaking requiring years of study and planning. It was not a card the Americans could throw on the table on short notice. Moreover, many experts in both Panama and the United States believed that the best site for a new canal was in Panama.[33] Thus, the Panamanians were not rendered totally helpless by the prospect of a new canal.

Another factor that influenced Panama was the intense domestic pressure to reach a new agreement on the new Panamanian president, Marcos Robles. The January riots had aroused the Panamanian people, and Robles now found himself locked into a position of having to repeat former President Chiari's hard-line demands. When the new round of talks began in January 1965, the Panamanians proposed an agenda virtually identical to the one they had put forward in the spring of 1964: an end to the hated perpetuity clause of the 1903 treaty, a fixed date for the termination of that treaty, a dramatic reduction in the American presence in the Zone, joint U.S.-Panamanian administration of the Zone until the expiration of the new treaty, and greater financial remuneration for Panama.[34]

The two sides appeared to be making progress in September 1965, when they agreed on four key points. First, the United States pledged, for the first time, to abrogate the 1903 treaty; second, a new treaty would recognize Panama's sovereignty over the Canal Zone; third, Panama was to become a partner with the United States in the administration and operation of the Canal; and finally, the United States would retain the right to defend the old Canal and any new canal constructed in Panama.[35] These points of agreement would guide the negotiations over the next two years.

But over the next two years the Panamanian government became increasingly weakened internally. The Robles administration, based on a loose coalition among a number of factions, had never been particularly strong. Panamanians on both the left and the right began to pressure the government to reach an agreement. The opposition press accused the Panamanian negotiating team of incompetence.[36] Robles was becoming desperate for an agreement. He had reduced his major demands to two: recognition of Panamanian sovereignty over the Canal and increased Panamanian share in revenues from the Canal tolls.

Robles's uncomfortable position was reflected in the formula reached in June 1967. This formula was in the form of three draft treaties, based on the agreed points of September 1965. The first treaty was designed to meet Panama's major demands. It provided for abrogation of the 1903 treaty, joint administration of the Canal by a Board of Directors composed of five Americans and four Panamanians, and an increase in toll revenue for Panama. The treaty was to expire on December 31, 1999, unless a new sea-level canal was completed earlier, in which case it would expire one year after the opening of the new canal. The final provision ended the perpetuity clause. The second draft treaty provided for joint U.S.-Panamanian defense of the Canal until the year 2004. If the United States built a new canal, the defense treaty would apply to both canals and would be extended to the year 2067. The final treaty gave the United States the right to build a new canal in Panama within the next twenty years, and to operate that canal for sixty years.[37]

These draft treaties reflect the American issue power position. While granting Panama sovereignty over the Canal and an end to the perpetuity clause, the treaties nevertheless contained many advantages for the United States. The joint administration provision was paid only lip service. Since the United States would have voting control on the Board of Directors, it would continue to have the final say in Canal administration. The defense treaty, one of the major American objectives in a new agreement, was designed to extend for up to one hundred years.

Robles came under fire almost immediately from domestic critics, who charged him with conceding too much. Particularly rankling to the Panamanians was their minority status on the Canal Board of Directors. This clause struck many as an example of American perfidy, since it would essentially maintain the status quo. Panama's negotiators admitted that the draft treaties were far from perfect, but argued that at least the country had "approached" its maximum goals. Moreover, they pointed out that as long as the United States maintained the option of building a new canal elsewhere, Panama had no choice but to mini-mize its demands.[38]

The Panamanian public did not accept the government's arguments. Robles, increasingly beleaguered, said the draft treaties would have to be "improved and modified."[39] But it was too late. In March 1968, the Panamanian National Assembly voted to oust Robles and replace him with the vice-president. Robles, however, refused to step down, and for several months Panama had two presidents. The ensuing political and constitutional crisis culminated in a coup d'état by Omar Torrijos in October 1968.

The 1967 draft treaties effectively died on the day they were an-nounced. The problem with this formula was that it exchanged de jure recognition of Panamanian sovereignty for de facto continued Ameri-can control, and thus did not satisfactorily deal with the question of Panamanian sovereignty over the Canal, which was, after all, the major issue in the negotiations. Although it officially abrogated the 1903 trea-ty, its handling of the defense and joint administration problems was so favorable to the United States as to make a mockery of Panamanian sovereignty. This flaw in the 1967 formula was all too obvious to Presi-dent Robles's political foes in Panama, who proceeded to orchestrate his ouster.

Why were the 1967 draft treaties so favorable to the United States? Stung by the January 1964 riots, the United States had sought to strengthen its issue power position by developing the alternative of building a new canal. The enhanced American position was reflected in the 1967 formula. The possibility that the United States might con-struct a new canal elsewhere in Central America limited the ability of the Panamanian negotiators to make demands.

But the ultimate effect of the U.S. tactic was not so favorable. Hard-line tactics against a weak government can backfire, for they may de-stroy the legitimacy of that government among its own people, and thus its ability to carry out the terms of agreement. This is precisely what happened in Panama. The 1967 draft treaties, which in the words of one analyst "did not differ significantly from Theodore Roosevelt's ap-proach,"[40] led to the fall not only of the Robles government but of Panama's democratic political system as well. The government of Omar Torrijos was to prove to be considerably more unified and effec-tive in negotiating with the Americans.

At the beginning of the Torrijos era, the negotiations had essentially returned to square one. Three years of bargaining had produced a formula that proved unacceptable to one of the sides. It was an un-acceptable formula because it was not a "resolving" formula; that is, it did not resolve the overriding problem of sovereignty. Zartman writes that, even if two parties agree on a formula, agreement does not necessarily make it a viable formula: "[An] agreement between parties is not enough. The formula must satisfy the demands of the conflict as well if it is to be a resolving formula."[41]

The negotiations returned to a diagnostic phase during the next several years when memory of the 1964 crisis loomed large in the calculations of both sides, thus keeping the pressure for renewed negotiations moderately strong.

But it was not simply the memory of the 1964 crisis that preserved the urge for negotiations. The issue power balance in 1967 was radically different from what it had been in early 1964. The Panamanians, by rejecting the 1967 draft treaties, had strongly communicated their great commitment to real changes in the Canal treaty. The fall of the Robles government largely because of popular disapproval of the formula indicated that minor concessions alone from the United States would no longer be acceptable to Panama. That the Panamanians risked provoking the Americans into playing their powerful card (constructing a new canal) further indicated the intensity of their commitment. This intensity, with the underlying threat of violence, was to be a major source of Panama's issue power over the next ten years.

Communicating Tactics, 1

Chiari's tactic of exploiting the 1964 riots by breaking diplomatic relations with the United States was only partly successful. It led to negotiations for a new treaty, but the result of these negotiations was an untenable formula. The Panamanian tactic was communicated at the highest level—Chiari's telephone conversations with President Johnson—and with deep commitment and passion. The problem was that the tactic lacked credibility. Panama did not have the structural power resources to allow it to sever relations with the United States for an extended period. Moreover, it was unlikely that Chiari was willing to allow further violent incidents to occur. The United States, after all, had responded forcefully to the January riots. Thus, the ultimate result of Chiari's tactic—the threat of more violence in the Canal Zone—could not be communicated credibly.

The United States, aware of Panama's structural power limitations, was never convinced that Chiari could pursue his tactic for very long, and was willing to wait for him to give in. But Panama did succeed in persuading the United States to change its perception of the situation. President Johnson agreed to begin negotiations over a new treaty because he believed that the status quo in Panama could no longer be maintained. But Johnson was influenced by the riots, not by Chiari's exploitation of them, except to the extent that his tactics kept Panama, and the memory of the riots, on the Johnson administration's agenda.

Thus, though Chiari's tactic lacked credibility, the riots themselves altered the U.S. perception of the situation. This explains the seemingly contradictory outcome in which the United States refused publicly to meet Chiari's demands while simultaneously preparing to meet them as soon as he backed down.

The American hard-line tactic of refusing to give in so long as Chiari refused to reestablish diplomatic relations succeeded. For one, it was a credible tactic; the United States would survive without a Panamanian ambassador in Washington. Further, the tactic was repeatedly communicated at the highest level. And it was combined with a carrot: the promise that the Canal issue would be discussed as soon as relations were reestablished.

Another key to the tactic's success is that it changed Panama's perception of the crisis. In the immediate aftermath of the January riots, Panama hoped that the United States could be quickly brought to the negotiation table. The severing of relations was not expected to continue for the long term. Exploiting the riots in this manner was only intended to prod the United States into action. When the United States instead adopted its hard-line tactic, Panama was gradually persuaded to see that the situation was not so favorable as it had thought. The United States was not going to back down quickly.

The Americans' other tactic during this period—the threat to build another canal—also succeeded. This threat was communicated to Panama in a number of ways, subtly at first (the leaked Pentagon study), but more directly later. In September 1964, Congress formally established the Atlantic-Pacific Interoceanic Canal Study Commission, and in December, Johnson publicly proclaimed a new canal as one of America's goals in the upcoming negotiations.[42]

The threat to build a new canal elsewhere in Central America was not 100 percent credible; the cost was undetermined, and it was unclear where a new canal would be built. But the threat was sufficiently credible to affect Panama's behavior greatly. After all, the United States did possess immense economic and technological resources, and no one was willing to bet much that the United States could *not* build a new canal.

The threat of a new canal changed Panama's perceptions of what it could get out of the negotiations. Its preferred outcome was pushed aside by the perceived need to appease the United States. Panama's objective changed from "how much can we get from the United States?" to "how much can we get from the United States without provoking them to build a new canal?"

sides' minds for the past six-and-one-half years, was now openly and forcefully stated by Torrijos.

Although Nixon's formula proposal played a large role in encouraging this new threat tactic by Panama, other factors were at work as well. For one, the United States was at this time in the throes of a painful and seemingly endless war in Vietnam. The U.S. dollar was under attack in world financial markets, and the American economy in general was less robust and less dominant than it had been just five years earlier. These factors helped to create the impression that American structural power was waning, and that America's commitment to foreign interests was weakening. Faced with domestic protests over the war in Vietnam, the American government was not likely to commit itself to military involvement in another foreign arena. This situation, even if based only on perception, served to weaken both America's apparent commitment to maintaining control of the Canal and the danger that America would respond to Panamanian threats by activating the military component of its structural power.

Another factor encouraging Panama's tactic derived from domestic sources. The Torrijos government was suffering through a period of internal attacks. Wealthy landowners were furious over land expropriations; business interests were frustrated by a stagnant economy; and the powerful Catholic Church was upset over the kidnapping of a progressive young priest, a deed rumored to have been carried out by the Torrijos-led National Guard. Torrijos was therefore eager to promote a unifying issue around which he could rally support. Nothing in Panamanian politics played this role better than the Canal issue.

By making thinly veiled threats of violence, Torrijos was placing himself in the potentially dangerous position of having to carry them out to save face. Yet one should not assume that Torrijos was unaware of this danger. Indeed, purposefully painting oneself into a corner is a potent means of demonstrating commitment.[53] Torrijos was trying to signal the United States that if necessary he was willing to place himself in a politically risky position to achieve his preferred outcome.

The Americans responded to Torrijos's threats by effectively rescinding the Nixon formula. The United States acknowledged that it was unwilling to confront a violent Panamanian attempt to secure its objectives. Thus, Torrijos's threat tactic was successful, something the general would not soon forget, whereas Nixon's hard-line tactic backfired miserably, thus diminishing the U.S. commitment. This course of events had a profound effect on the issue power balance.

Two days after Torrijos's fiery October speech, the United States acknowledged that it would agree to drop the perpetuity clause and work for a new treaty with a fixed termination date. The Nixon administration, however, insisted that whatever the outcome of the ongoing talks, the United States would maintain the right to operate and defend the waterway "for a very long time," and the right either to improve the existing canal or to build a new one. Other administration sources said that American troops would be "permanently" stationed in the Zone.[54] The only kind word from the Americans concerned increased economic benefits for Panama. But the Panamanians perceived the offer of greater aid not as generosity. In the words of a close observer: "[I]t smelled strongly of a payoff"; that is, the United States appeared willing to help Torrijos end his country's economic woes in exchange for a less strident Panamanian position on the Canal.[55]

Despite its own economic troubles, the costly war in Vietnam and the failed formula, the Nixon administration was not prepared to give in easily to Panamanian threats. In fact, acknowledged perception of America's new weakness may have encouraged American policy makers to maintain an essentially hard-line position in the negotiations with Panama. Although the United States had backed down on the question of a termination date for a new treaty, it continued to demand a formula providing administrative rights for a considerable length of time and military defense rights indefinitely The negotiations were stalemated throughout much of 1972.

By the middle of 1972, Torrijos had become convinced that the United States was not going to be more forthcoming in negotiations. Although unsuccessful, Nixon's formula in the summer of 1971 had revealed the nature of the American administration's heart. Congress's heart was equally cold to Panama's position. Of the thirty-six senators and representatives who had made statements during two days of congressional hearings held in September 1971, only one, Senator Alan Cranston of California, endorsed negotiations.[56] Torrijos's threats in late 1971 persuaded the Americans to accept once and for all a fixed termination date on any new treaty. But beyond that concession (a concession that had in fact been offered in 1967 by President Johnson) the United States did not seem willing to move.

Despite the hard line taken by the United States, the issue power balance had shifted noticeably toward Panama. The Canal Commission's report had revealed that the United States had no alternatives outside of Panama; the success of Torrijos's threats in confronting the American proposal had indicated the great commitment of the Panamanians to secure their objectives; and contextual events—the Vietnam War, the weakened American economy—had raised questions about the U.S. ability and commitment to achieving its desired outcome unilaterally.

Yet, the issue power balance had not shifted sufficiently to allow for any further progress in the negotiations. Throughout most of 1972, the United States showed that it could practically ignore the Canal issue. To get the negotiations moving again, the Panamanians would have to develop a tactic to alter the issue power balance even more in their favor. One way to do so would have been to activate the ever-present Panamanian potential to challenge American control of the Canal—in other words, to carry out Torrijos's threats of violence.

It would have been quite easy for the Panamanian government to prompt such violence, but it would have been a risky tactic. Threatening violence is an effective tactic for encouraging the opponent to make concessions in negotiations; actually carrying out violence risks causing a break-off of negotiations, perhaps permanently. Because Torrijos felt that the best chance for resolving the Canal issue was through negotiation, he did not want to risk causing an end to the negotiation process.

Another, less risky, tactic open to Panama would also serve to alter the issue power balance. Throughout 1971 and 1972, Torrijos began to consult regularly with leaders of neighboring Latin American countries, particularly U.S. allies such as Colombia, Venezuela, and Costa Rica, but also with Peru and Cuba.[57] The purpose of these consultations was to begin to develop the tactic of coalition building and internationalization of the Canal issue. Until this point, Panama had stood virtually alone in its negotiations with the United States; Torrijos now was developing allies.

When it was finally clear that the talks with the Nixon administration were not going to prove fruitful, Panama activated its tactic of internationalization of the Canal issue. Torrijos had been working on this for some time in consultation with fellow Latin American leaders. He was now prepared to move the issue on to the world stage.

In November 1972, Panama's chief delegate to the United Nations formally requested that the United Nations Security Council meet in Panama so the world community could witness firsthand "the inequities Panama has endured."[58] The United States opposed such a meeting outside the U.N. headquarters in New York. The Americans argued that the Canal problem was a bilateral one, and should not be the focus of a Security Council meeting. But with impressive support from Latin American and other Third World delegates, support he had been courting for some time, Torrijos succeeded. The United Nations agreed to convene a Security Council meeting in Panama in March 1973.

The meeting was a major success for Torrijos. He adroitly walked a thin line. He ensured that there were no violent anti-American demonstrations in the streets, while simultaneously warning in a speech to the Security Council delegates that "violent changes" would occur if "the colony in the heart of my country" was not removed. He called the American position "absurd," while pledging to continue working for a "just and fair treaty." In the end, Panama and Peru proposed a Security Council resolution urging the United States and Panama to conclude a new treaty "without delay" that would "fulfill Panama's legitimate aspiration and guarantee full respect for Panama's effective sovereignty over all its territory."[59] To its dismay, the U.S. delegation found itself alone in casting a negative vote (the United Kingdom abstained, and the other thirteen members of the Council voted in favor of the resolution).

The Americans were stung. Only two years earlier, they had felt their issue power position was sufficiently secure to warrant proposing a hard-line formula. Now, the Panamanians had successfully turned the world spotlight on the Canal issue and demonstrated the degree to which they had rallied support for their position. This broadened the base of Panama's commitment by transforming the Canal question into a North-South issue. It was no longer simply Panama versus the United States; it was now the "colonized" versus the "colonizer." The stark tally of the Security Council vote—thirteen to one against the United States—while only symbolic, presented a picture of a surrounded United States, facing the near unanimous opposition of world opinion. Panama's commitment was greatly intensified by adding to it the commitment of many others.

Moreover, by speaking of the Canal issue in terms of "colonizer" and "colonized," Panama was bringing to its cause the principles of the anticolonial movement. The United States, which had hitherto been, for the most part, spared the accusation of being a colonizer, found itself in an awkward position. As the self-appointed leader of the "free world," the United States feared for its image in the developing countries, an image already tarnished by the war in Vietnam. In a sense, this new threat to America's image was potentially more dangerous than that caused by the Vietnam War. For this new accusation came from the very hemisphere the United States had until then considered to be outside the realm of the East-West struggle (with the notable exception of Cuba). One commentator noted that the effect on the United States of the Security Council resolution was similar to the effect an outburst of violence in Eastern Europe would have had on the Soviet Union.[60]

Stephen S. Rosenfeld described the impact of the Security Council meeting on U.S. policy: "The propaganda and political beating administered in the United Nations helped transform the issue within the U.S. government from a modest regional matter, which could safely be left in a state of stagnation, into a major priority."[61]

In congressional testimony in April 1973, Ambassador David H. Ward, the U.S. special representative for Inter-Oceanic Canal Negotiations, supported this view: "We are not going to pick up our marbles and go home because of the Security Council meeting, but I think it did have the effect of raising questions in the mind of people in this country, and in the mind of the President, and in the mind of Congress as to just exactly how can we work this problem out."[62]

American U.N. Ambassador John A. Scali, also in testimony before Congress, noted the success of the Security Council meeting in transforming the Canal issue from a bilateral one into a regional one: "[The United States] may have vetoed the resolution, but Latin America has vetoed the United States."[63] At the same hearings, Congressman Donald Fraser, Minnesota Democrat, expressed what he felt were the implications of the Security Council vote: "The fact [is] we lost. We were the only one to stand up on our side. Even our closest ally [Britain], a conservative government, did not stand with us. It seems to me we ought to get this negotiation completed."[64]

In sum, the Security Council meeting in Panama led to a critical change in the Nixon administration's perception of the issue. Before the meeting, "the Nixon administration would have preferred the canal negotiations to fail rather than accept unwanted compromises." After the meeting, "a compromise agreement was preferred to deadlock because continuation of the status quo was seen as threatening the efficient operation and security of the Canal."[65]

William Furlong and Margaret Scranton point to another important consequence of the Security Council meeting:

> Panama's strategy focused the attention of a broader group and higher level of policymakers on the Canal issue. This altered the personnel involved with Canal policy from a small, insulated group of experts on the Panama Canal and its defense . . . to a larger group including National Security Adviser Kissinger and State Department officials with experience in Latin America, hemispheric affairs and Panama.[66]

That Panama was now in a much stronger issue power position, and that the United States recognized this, became evident just two months after the special Security Council meeting. In his annual report to Congress on the state of U.S. foreign policy, President Nixon wrote in May 1973:

> Another important unresolved problem concerns the Panama Canal and the surrounding Zone. U.S. operation of the Canal and our presence in Panama are governed by the terms of a treaty drafted in 1903. The world has changed radically during the 70 years this treaty has been in effect. Latin America has changed. Panama has changed. And the terms of our relationship should reflect those changes in a reasonable way.
>
> For the past nine years, efforts to work out a new treaty acceptable to both

parties have failed. That failure has put considerable strain on our relations with Panama. It is time for both parties to take a fresh look at this problem and to develop a new relationship between us—one that will guarantee continued effective operation of the Canal while meeting Panama's legitimate aspirations.[67]

This statement represented a new "turning point of seriousness." As in December 1964, the United States once again was acknowledging that it was prepared to make concessions in order to bring about a negotiated solution to the Canal problem. The way was now prepared for a serious search for a new formula.

The coming to power of Omar Torrijos in Panama had marked a significant change in the issue power balance. Torrijos demonstrated early that he was not afraid to use the threat of violence to elicit concessions from the Americans. He knew that the memory of the 1964 riots—and what they implied about the security of the Canal—was not far in the back of the minds of the Americans. At the same time, he was careful to avoid any actualization of this threat. His effective control over the Panamanian National Guard ensured that there would be no organized violence without his consent.

Torrijos also saw the benefit of internationalizing the Canal issue, and he used this tactic masterfully. In Torrijos's words, "to resolve a problem, the first thing you have to do is *make* it a problem."[68] He knew that in the preceding years the Canal issue had been a problem for the United States only sporadically; for example, during the 1964 riots. He also knew that he could usefully latch on to trends operating in the world in order to make the Canal issue a more enduring problem for the Americans. The first step in this tactic was the U.N. meeting in Panama.

The resulting turning point of seriousness was significant for two reasons: First, it came from a right-wing American administration which, just two years earlier, had clumsily attempted to bluff its way out of continuing the negotiations. Second, it came as a result of a substantial and apparently permanent shift in the issue power balance in Panama's favor. The 1964 riots had caused enough of a shift in the issue power balance to bring about Johnson's concessions later that year. But that shift lacked an enduring quality, especially as the shock caused by the riots gradually passed. Furthermore, at that time, the United States still possessed the option of building a new canal, and threatened to do so outside of Panama. This option corrected somewhat the shift in power brought about by the riots. But by 1973, the new tactics orchestrated by Torrijos, combined with the Canal Commission's report (which undermined the American alternative), had led to a more enduring shift in the issue power balance.

By the end of 1973, certain contextual events helped shift the balance even further in Panama's favor. The American defeat in Vietnam was apparent to all; it was now clear that, with sufficient commitment to its cause, the weak could defeat the strong. The crisis caused by the Arab states' oil embargo during the 1973 Arab-Israeli war greatly boosted Panama's optimism, and created a sense of unity among all Third World nations. It conveniently coincided with Panama's tactic of internationalizing the Canal debate. It also provided the Panamanians with a persuasive analogy: Just as OPEC (Organization of Petroleum Exporting Countries) was justified in reaping the benefits from the oil in its ground, so Panama was justified in reaping the benefits from its primary "natural resource," the Canal.

Thus, the renewed turning point of seriousness in May 1973 was based on a fundamental change in the issue power balance. In the prototype negotiation process described by Zartman and Berman, a turning point of seriousness is followed by a search for a formula. The 1967 draft treaties can be seen as the formula that resulted from the December 1964 turning point. Unfortunately, it was a formula unacceptable to the Panamanians. This failure had led to a return to square one, new attempts by both sides to alter the issue power balance, and, as explained above, a new turning point of seriousness in May 1973. What was needed at this point was a new formula.

Nixon's report to Congress had an immediate impact on the Panamanian leadership. Torrijos, who correctly perceived it as a serious turning point in the stalled negotiations, directed his foreign minister, Juan Antonio Tack, to draft a response. Tack pondered Nixon's statement for several weeks, and finally determined that the appropriate response was a Panamanian statement of principles—in other words, a formula proposal.

In a nine-page letter to U.S. Secretary of State William P. Rogers, Tack presented the Panamanian view of an acceptable formula. This view was embodied in eight points:

1. The 1903 treaty must be abrogated.
2. A new treaty must have a fixed termination date.
3. U.S. jurisdiction in any part of Panama should end.
4. The United States could use land and water areas necessary to operate and maintain the Canal and to protect vital installations.
5. Panama must receive "a just and equitable share" in Canal benefits.

6. U.S. government activities should be limited to operating, maintaining, and protecting the Canal.
7. Military activities could be only those "expressly stipulated in the treaty."
8. The United States would have the right to build a sea-level canal if (a) the U.S. decision was made within "a reasonable period," (b) Panama retained full jurisdiction in the new canal area, and (c) a sea-level canal treaty also had a fixed termination date.[69]

In the fall, Tack's letter was passed on to Henry Kissinger, who had assumed the top job at the State Department. Though normally more concerned with the "high politics" of East-West relations, Kissinger took a special interest in the Canal negotiations. He had been rudely awakened to the problem by the Security Council meeting in Panama, and particularly by the lone stand of the United States in vetoing the Panamanian resolution.[70] His determination to solve the problem quickly was evidenced in his choice of veteran diplomat Ellsworth Bunker to be the new chief U.S. negotiator. After consulting with officials in the State Department and Pentagon, Bunker developed his own set of principles, which closely resembled Tack's, but differed in the way U.S. defense rights were described. Bunker was dispatched to Panama in November 1973 to begin negotiating a new formula (or "set of principles," as Kissinger described it) on the basis of Tack's letter and Bunker's draft response.

Progress was rapid. By early December agreement had been reached on most of Tack's points. After a brief visit to Washington for consultations, Bunker returned in early January to Panama where he and Tack completed the job. In February, Kissinger—never one to shun the limelight—flew to Panama to sign formally the joint statement of principles Bunker and Tack had negotiated. The Kissinger-Tack formula consisted essentially of the eight points Tack had made in his letter. It exchanged American agreement to eliminate the perpetuity clause of the 1903 treaty for vaguely worded assurances that the United States would continue to play a role in Canal defense. This vagueness was intentional. The parties knew that the question of U.S. defense rights was the most potentially controversial issue, to be dealt with in detail only after other issues had been resolved and the negotiations had gained some momentum.[71] The following were the main features of the agreement:

1. The 1903 treaty would be abrogated by the conclusion of an entirely new treaty.
2. The concept of perpetuity would be eliminated; the new treaty would have a fixed termination date.
3. Termination of United States jurisdiction over Panamanian ter-

ritory would take place promptly in accordance with the terms of a new treaty.

4. The Panamanian territory in which the Canal is situated would return to Panamanian jurisdiction, though for the duration of the new treaty the United States would have certain land, water, and airspace rights necessary for operation, maintenance, and defense of the Canal.

5. Panama would receive a "just and equitable" share of benefits derived from the Canal.

6. Panama would participate in the administration of the Canal until expiration of the new treaty, and would assume sole responsibility for Canal administration after this point.

7. Panama would participate with the United States in the protection and defense of the Canal.

8. The United States and Panama would agree bilaterally on provisions for enlarging Canal capacity.[72]

In his public remarks at the signing ceremony in Panama City, Kissinger made an interesting observation: "In the past, our negotiations would have been determined by relative strength. Today we have come together in an act of reconciliation."[73] It can be assumed that Kissinger was referring to what we have termed aggregate structural power. But as has been emphasized, it is issue power that determines the course and outcome of negotiations. And in terms of issue power, relative strength had shifted to Panama.

A comparison of the 1974 Kissinger-Tack formula with the 1967 formula (as embodied in the draft treaties of that year) reveals the degree to which the issue power balance had shifted in Panama's favor during the intervening seven years. Gone from the 1974 formula were (1) U.S. predominance, via the five-to-four advantage on the Board of Directors, in administration of the Canal; (2) the extensive American defense rights of the 1967 draft treaties, which would have given the United States chief defense responsibilities until, potentially, the year 2067; and (3) the American right to make the unilateral decision to build a new canal. Although the Kissinger-Tack formula was vague on many points points (that is the nature of formulas), unlike the 1967 formula, it was nevertheless one that Panama could live with. For the first time since the 1964 crisis the parties had a mutually agreed-upon basis to begin negotiating the details of an agreement.

The Detail Phase and the Outcome

Three principal issues were to dominate the detail stage of the negotiations: (1) the duration of a new Canal treaty (i.e., how long the United

States would continue to have rights in the Canal Zone before complete sovereignty passed to Panama); (2) preservation of the Canal's neutrality after control passed to Panama; and (3) U.S. defense rights in the Zone during the life and after the expiration of the new treaty. A fourth issue, the amount of financial remuneration Panama would receive under the new treaty, briefly became the focus of attention during the final weeks of the negotiations. As in the formula stage of the negotiations, each side's tactics during the detail stage were directed toward affecting the issue power balance in such a way as to promote its favored outcome in the above issue areas.

It was not tactics alone, however, that affected the issue power positions of the two sides in the detail stage. Two critical contextual factors also had an impact on the power balance, both to the general detriment of Panama. The first was the politicization of the Canal issue in the United States, notably during the 1976 presidential elections. The second was Panama's deteriorating economic condition and growing social unrest. The Torrijos government was to spend much of its time during the detail stage devising tactics to counter the detrimental impact of these two contextual factors.

Kissinger's public appearance in Panama to sign the formula agreement had the unintended side effect of introducing the American public to the Canal issue. Barely a month after the Kissinger-Tack formula had been signed, thirty-eight senators—four more than the number needed to block a treaty—voted in favor of a Strom Thurmond–authored resolution opposing giving sovereignty over the Canal to Panama.[74] President Nixon, facing a possible impeachment trial, was reluctant to antagonize conservative members of Congress. He allowed the negotiations to stall.

After President Ford's succession to the White House in the summer of 1974, negotiations were renewed more vigorously. For a brief period in early 1975, Torrijos appeared optimistic, telling the *New York Times* that the United States had finally accepted the need to resolve the Canal issue.[75] Before long, however, the question of treaty duration surfaced as a major conflict. The U.S. negotiators, under pressure from the Pentagon, were demanding a fifty-year duration for the new treaty; Panama insisted the treaty must expire before the year 2000.

Meanwhile, more trouble was brewing on Capitol Hill. Kentucky Congressman Gene Snyder proposed an amendment to a State Department appropriations bill that would withhold funds for "negotiating the surrender" of U.S. rights in the Canal Zone. The amendment won overwhelmingly, 246 to 164.[76] The Senate later rejected the Snyder amendment, but the lesson was not lost on Ford and Kissinger. Ronald Reagan was already positioning himself to challenge Ford for the Republican nomination, and had adopted the antinegotiation position as one of the themes of his vitriolic campaign. The result of this political pressure, combined with the Pentagon's strong opposition to concessions, led to a hardening of the U.S. position. In September 1975, Henry Kissinger declared in a speech to southern governors that "[t]he United States must maintain the right, unilaterally, to defend the Panama Canal for an indefinite future."[77]

In July 1975, Torrijos, already frustrated by the American political situation, had said that if negotiations ended violence would be inevitable: "Two courses of action would be open to me. To smash it [the uprising] or to lead it, and I am not going to smash it."[78] Kissinger's unfortunate remark, which reneged on one of the points of agreement reached with Tack, provided Torrijos the opportunity to demonstrate his seriousness. With Torrijos's permission, if not on his command, several hundred Panamanians besieged the U.S. embassy in Panama City while National Guardsmen looked on approvingly.[79] The furor subsided after several days, and after Kissinger recanted some of his remarks. Torrijos had thus demonstrated what a powerful tactic the threat of violence was.

But Torrijos's threat also revealed the degree to which he felt his power position deteriorating. The antinegotiation movement in the United States was weakening American commitment to reaching an agreement. Moreover, the specter of a possible Reagan nomination and election to the presidency was increasing the possibility that the United States might soon return to a policy of achieving unilateral outcomes in Central America. The U.S.-Panamanian consensus, epitomized in the Kissinger-Tack formula, appeared to be unraveling as a result of U.S. politics. Torrijos resorted to his threat tactic in order to bolster Panama's position.

In early 1976, Torrijos renewed his earlier successful tactic of coalition building, this time by paying a state visit to Cuba. This trip not only enhanced Panama's standing among the nonaligned nations, it also served as a threat: If the United States were not forthcoming, Panama could turn to another "bloc." Torrijos also successfully persuaded Argentina to defer its claim to a seat on the Security Council, passing it to Panama, thus securing a prominent platform from which to voice his position.

Torrijos's tactics had a noticeable effect. In March 1976, Kissinger warned that, if no agreement were reached, "the danger we see is that the countries of the hemisphere will unite in a policy of harassment" against the United States.[80] Within several weeks, however, Ronald Reagan had won a string of primaries, and his challenge to President Ford became a serious threat. Once again, the antinegotiation forces seemed to be gaining the upper hand in American politics. President Ford responded by hardening his own position on the Canal issue, but at the expense of undermining the Kissinger-Tack formula and making the job of his negotiators more difficult.

Torrijos was in a bind. Angered over the American administration's waffling, he was nevertheless frightened by the prospect of a Reagan victory. He had to find a way to keep the pressure on Ford without increasing Reagan's popularity. Torrijos's discomfort grew even more when Jimmy Carter, the candidate who clearly would win the Democratic nomination, tried to position himself somewhere between Ford and Reagan. In a June speech before the New York Foreign Policy Association, Carter said, "I would never give up full control of the Panama Canal as long as it had any contribution to make to our own national security."[81]

Torrijos's tactics during this period were evidence of his confusion over how to approach the negotiations. On the one hand, he called for his fellow Panamanians to be patient, and not to do anything that might play into the hands of Reagan.[82] Yet, he also resorted periodically to his earlier tactic of threat making and coalition building. In a speech before the Conference of Non-Aligned Nations in Sri Lanka, he blasted the United States for maintaining a "colonial enclave" in his country, and sought greater Third World endorsement of Panama's position.[83]

The other contextual factor that weakened Panama's issue power position was the rapidly deteriorating state of the country's economy, resulting in signs of social unrest. The Panamanian economy showed a zero growth rate in 1976. The inflation rate was high and exports were falling as foreign debt mounted. For several years, Torrijos had used the Canal issue as a shield against domestic opposition to his regime and its failing economic policies. Criticizing Torrijos over any issue had been regarded as tantamount to betraying Panama over the Canal. But with the negotiations in recess pending the outcome of the U.S. elections, opposition groups began to voice their discontent more openly. Torrijos needed a Canal agreement, and he needed it soon. When in April 1976 Torrijos warned that trouble would erupt if the treaty were not signed by 1977, he was in part threatening and in part pleading.

The Panamanians regarded Jimmy Carter's election to the presidency warily because of the ambiguous position he had taken during the campaign. But their concern quickly turned to optimism. Several weeks before his inauguration, Carter said at a press conference that the Panama problem "ought to be resolved quite rapidly."[84] His Secretary of State–designate Cyrus Vance also publicly stressed the importance of a Canal agreement.

Carter's commitment to resolving the Canal problem was based largely on his fears that the Panamanians might soon activate their threats. In his memoirs, Carter writes: "The Canal was in serious danger from direct attack and sabotage unless a new and fair treaty arrangement could be forged." He also reports that the commanding U.S. Army officer in the Canal Zone told him it would require "at least a hundred thousand armed men to mount a reasonable defense of the Canal within a hostile environment."[85]

Carter also expressed concern over how the continuing stalemate in the Canal negotiations would affect U.S. relations with the rest of the Third World: "This issue had become a litmus test throughout the world, indicating how the United States, as a superpower, would treat a small and relatively defenseless nation."[86]

Panamanian optimism received a further boost when, in January 1977, Carter appointed Sol Linowitz to be co-negotiator with Ellsworth Bunker. Linowitz had headed the privately funded Commission on United States–Latin American Relations whose recent report had recommended early completion of a new Canal treaty.[87] Suddenly, the United States was recommitted to a quick and equitable solution.

In light of Torrijos's eroded issue power position, it may at first seem odd that the United States was increasing its commitment to negotiations. After all, Panama's weakened issue power should have allowed the United States to harden its position, perhaps by formally abrogating parts of the Kissinger-Tack formula. But the reality was more complex. For one thing, Torrijos's domestic troubles had become an indirect source of Panamanian power. Many American officials, particularly at the Department of State, felt that Torrijos was the one Panamanian leader most capable of negotiating a new accord. In their view, if Torrijos fell, the alternative probably would be a government even further to the left, which might harden the Panamanian position or even encourage popular unrest. As Zbigniew Brzezinski later wrote: "A delay in negotiating a treaty invited violence and also endangered Torrijos's position; and Panama without Torrijos most likely would have been an impossible negotiating partner."[88] The 1964 riots still cast an ominous shadow.

Moreover, Torrijos's unrelenting efforts at coalition building were paying off. Soon after his inauguration, President Carter received a letter from the leaders of Colombia, Costa Rica, Guatemala, Honduras, Mexico, Nicaragua, and Venezuela, in which they pledged that a new Canal treaty would be the "crucial test of the degree of sincerity of the inter-American policy of the United States."[89] It struck a sharp chord in a president who wanted to focus American foreign policy more toward the Third World. In this sense, the American commitment to a Canal treaty had increased with the election of Carter, not so much because of any specific tactics on the part of Panama, but because of the ideological views of the new administration.

Thus, the ironic result of the heated U.S. presidential campaign was an issue power balance more in Panama's favor. The damage caused to Torrijos's internal position by the U.S. campaign's rhetoric had only emphasized the possible negative consequences of his overthrow. This fact, combined with the more liberal ideological views of the new Carter administration, led to increased American commitment. Yet, as will be seen, the strengthened Panamanian issue power position was only a temporarily beneficial result of Torrijos's problems. As the negotiations over details proceeded, his problems would begin to affect negatively Panama's position.

What would prove to be the final round of the talks began in February 1977. Two fundamental details remained to be worked out: the termination date of the new treaty and the matter of access to and defense of the Canal after the new treaty was in force. U.S. negotiators were asking for a twenty-to-fifty-year period before termination of the treaty; the Panamanians insisted that the treaty terminate, and control of the Canal pass to Panama, by the year 2000.

The more critical question was what rights, if any, the United States would have to ensure access to and defense of the Canal after expiration of the new treaty. Panama refused to grant the United States exclusive rights to intervene once the new treaty had expired. Torrijos proposed instead that guarantees of access and of Canal neutrality be vested in the United Nations. The Americans, however, maintained the position that, in the words of President Carter, "we would have an assured capacity or capability" to guarantee access to the Canal after the new treaty's expiration.[90]

The Americans' tough position on Canal defense derived from two sources. Carter knew that opposition by many senators to a new Canal treaty would be fierce. Without adequate guarantees that the United States would play a paramount role in Canal defense for the indefinite future, it was unlikely a new treaty would be ratified. Secretary of State Vance warned the Panamanians several times during the spring that the new treaty would have to be acceptable to at least sixty-seven senators.

The other source of the Americans' tough position, alluded to earlier, was the intensifying domestic pressure on Torrijos, which was leading to a deterioration in Panama's issue power position. Internal opposition to Torrijos was coming from all sides. Unions were angered over recent wage freezes; student activists had lost faith in Torrijos's revolutionary fervor; and the business community, never a source of regime support, had lost confidence in the government's ability to restore growth to the stagnant economy. Torrijos's need for a new Canal treaty was greater than ever, not only because a new treaty would end investors' fears of political unrest, but also because a new treaty would increase Panama's Canal revenues substantially above the current $2.3 million. Torrijos's alternatives were now virtually nonexistent; he needed a new treaty and he needed U.S. economic aid. The issue power balance had unmistakably shifted in the Americans' favor.

In May 1977, Bunker suggested a compromise solution to the defense rights problem. He proposed an informal understanding that would give Panama the task of defending the Canal from internal threats, and the United States the task of defending against external threats. The Panamanians accepted this proposal.[91] Making this position an informal understanding was merely a face-saving device for Panama. For in reality, this was a major concession by Torrijos. It meant that the United States would effectively enjoy the permanent right to defend the Canal. In return, the United States agreed to Panama's preferred expiration date, December 31, 1999.

By late July, the sole remaining issue was that of financial compensation. Torrijos had saved this issue for last. Though financial compensation had played only a minor role in the early years of the negotiations, it had increasingly become a crucial issue to the Panamanians, all the more so in light of their large concession on the defense issue.

With an agreement in sight, and President Carter anxious to achieve an early foreign policy success, Torrijos felt the time was ripe to push for a large financial reward. The U.S. offer was for a $50 million lump sum; Torrijos demanded a $1 billion lump sum plus a $300 million annuity for the life of the new treaty. The great disparity in positions caused a last-minute crisis in the negotiations. Zartman and Berman note that such extreme last-minute demands, after an agreement seems imminent, are typical of many negotiations.[92]

The financial issue was not resolved until Carter, in a personal letter to Torrijos, warned that further concessions by the United States would seriously threaten chances for Senate ratification. The United States did, however, agree to an increase in Panama's share of Canal toll revenues, amounting to $40 to $50 million a year. In addition, Carter promised $295 million in loans and guarantees over the next five years, and $50 million in military assistance over the next ten years.[93]

The United States and Panama reached agreement on a new Canal treaty on August 11, 1977.[94] The key points of the new agreement discussed above can be summarized as follows:

- The United States would continue to operate and defend the Canal until midnight, December 31, 1999. Panama, however, was to assume immediate territorial jurisdiction over the Canal and, over a three-year period, legal jurisdiction.
- American citizens living and working in the Canal Zone would be able to keep their jobs as long as they wished. They would be replaced by Panamanians only when they quit or retired.
- The United States would have primary responsibility to defend the Canal from external threats until the year 2000, and the permanent right to guarantee the Canal's neutrality.
- The United States would provide Panama the financial compensation discussed above.

Communicating Tactics, 2

President Nixon's hard-line formula proposal in the summer of 1971 proved to be a tactical mistake. It was neither credible nor effective in changing Panamanians' perceptions.

Part of the problem was the uncertainty about what kind of tactic it was: Was it an offer to Panama of better financial terms in lieu of sovereignty, a payoff? Or was it an effort to force a return to the pre-1964 status quo, a bluff?

As a payoff, it lacked credibility; no amount of money could buy Panamanian acquiescence. The issue was not money, but sovereignty. To be credible, a tactic must have the prospect of succeeding. A tactic that does not relate to the issues being negotiated—in this case, sovereignty—has little chance of changing either the other side's perceptions or its behavior.

If the tactic was a bluff, it also lacked credibility. The 1964 riots had changed Americans' perception of the situation. Specifically, they had persuaded the United States to accept that the status quo in Panama was no longer possible. Nothing occurred between 1964 and 1971 to change this perception. Thus, Nixon's tactic was not a credible bluff, based as it was on an outdated perception of the situation.

That Panama's perception did not change after the Nixon tactic is evidenced by Torrijos's immediate response. This response—the warnings of violence and the threats to break off the negotiations—was endowed with considerable credibility. Not only did Torrijos communicate his response unequivocally to the American negotiators, he also began a rhetorical campaign in Panama to impassion his people. By so doing, he was putting his own reputation and commitment on the line; he was, in fact, painting himself into a corner. As already noted, this can be an extremely effective way to bolster a tactic's credibility.

Panama's tactic was thus credible whereas America's was not. The outcome of this tactical exchange reflected this fact. The United States backed down and rescinded the Nixon formula. The objective of Panama's tactic had been to keep the United States doing what it had been doing, that is, perceiving the Canal issue as a problem of sovereignty. After over a year of stalemate, however, Torrijos found it necessary to adopt a new tactic to get the United States to do something different, specifically, to start moving forward in the negotiations.

Panama's tactic of coalition building, crowned by the United Nations Security Council meeting in Panama City, persuaded the United States of the need to renew the negotiation process. The tactic of coalition building, by its very nature, occurs outside of the bilateral negotiation process. It is thus an indirect communication, though hardly a subtle one.

Several things are necessary for a tactic of coalition building to be credible. First, and most obviously, other actors must be willing to join the coalition. Moreover, these actors must possess some leverage or influence over the other negotiator.

Second, the coalition partners must do something other than merely lend their name to the cause; otherwise, they will not be contributing to the negotiation process. Participation can range from joint coercive actions to symbolic demonstrations to quiet diplomacy. The more partners in the coalition, and the more influence they have over the opposing negotiator, the more effective their actions are likely to be.

Finally, the partners must share a common cause, ideology, or objective that binds the coalition together. Coalitions based purely on short-term expediency, such as the U.S.-Soviet alliance during World War II, are unlikely to survive a tedious negotiation process.

Torrijos's coalition of Latin American and other Third World nations was credible on all three counts. Many of its members possessed influence over the United States, particularly longtime American allies Mexico and Venezuela. And even those that did not possess much influence were nevertheless nations the United States did not want to alienate for fear that they would be lured into the Soviet bloc. Moreover, Torrijos was at times able to bring non–Third World nations into his coalition, such as during the vote at the Security Council meeting in Panama. These states possessed even greater influence over the United States.

Panama's coalition partners were also active in support of Panama's position. It was largely through their cooperation that Torrijos succeeded in bringing the Security Council meeting to Panama. In the fall of 1973, the foreign ministers of twenty-three Latin American states met in Colombia to prepare an agenda for U.S.–Latin American dialogue. Prominent on the list was the "solution to the Panama Canal question." Even during the detail phase of the negotiations Latin American leaders were in frequent communication with President Carter, both to encourage continued progress and to serve as a back channel between Carter and Torrijos.

Finally, Panama's coalition was united by an objective that transcended the Canal issue: a final end to the vestiges of colonialism. Panama and its partners felt that both justice and history were on their side; this belief was a powerful motivation. Because of it, the Canal issue was transformed into a symbolic struggle uniting nations that, individually, had nothing tangible at stake.

Torrijos's tactic of coalition building was thus endowed with great credibility. It changed the American perception of the issue from that of a bilateral U.S.-Panamanian problem to a more fundamental, and eventually inevitable, step in the historical process. It also changed U.S. behavior, the hallmark of a successful tactic.

By contrast, the last Panamanian tactic in the negotiation process—the eleventh-hour demand for greatly increased financial remuneration—was a failure. Because it lacked credibility, it was quickly seen as a bluff. It lacked credibility because it came at the end, after Panama had received much that it wanted and an agreement was in sight. The United States was not persuaded that Panama would risk all that it had gained by pushing hard for an unjustified financial reward. This is not to say that it was a bad tactic, or that Torrijos should not have attempted it. After all, it might have worked, and when it became apparent that it would not, it was easily retracted. And though it caused some anger among the U.S. negotiators, it did not cause them to retaliate or rescind any U.S. concessions.

Conclusions: Power and Tactics

Pivotal Events

Three pivotal events between 1964 and 1977 led to major changes in the issue power balance and thus largely determined the eventual outcome of the Canal negotiations. The first was the riots in January 1964. By demonstrating the degree to which Panama could control outcomes, or at least disrupt the Americans' ability to control outcomes, the riots forced U.S. policy makers to reassess their position on renegotiating the 1903 treaty. Specifically, the riots forced the United States to determine whether its most important objective was continued unilateral control of the Canal or continued secure operation of the Canal. The message of the 1964 riots was that the two objectives were mutually exclusive.

President Johnson's decision in late 1964 to renegotiate the 1903 treaty was an important victory for Panama, and indicative of the degree to which the issue power balance had shifted in Panama's favor. But by coupling this concession with the threat to build a new canal elsewhere in Central America, the United States tapped its great structural power advantage to increase its alternatives and thus largely corrected the deleterious change in the issue power balance. The result of this tactical exchange was the 1967 formula, which offered Panama only token sharing of control in exchange for de facto continued U.S. dominance. But because it dealt only cosmetically with the question of sovereignty, it proved unacceptable to the Panamanian body politic (even if it was acceptable to President Chiari) and was at least partially responsible for the ensuing political crisis and coup d'état in Panama.

There followed a lull in Canal negotiations because of both the political uncertainty in Panama and the election of a conservative administration in the United States. This lull was broken by the second pivotal event in the negotiations, the report of the Canal Study Commission in November 1970. This report revealed that the United States in fact had no alternatives other than Panama for achieving its objective of a secure interoceanic canal. The initial American response was to harden its position, the Nixon formula proposal of 1971. But the Panamanians, aware of how the Canal Commission's report had altered the issue power balance to their advantage, initiated a tactic of threats and warnings, harking back to the 1964 riots. The immediate impact of this tactic was an American concession: the repudiation of the Nixon formula. The threats and warnings tactic was not, however, successful in bringing about a renewal of serious negotiations.

It took another Panamanian tactic to accomplish that, the tactic of coalition building and internationalization of the Canal issue, most evident in the 1973 United Nations Security Council meeting in Panama City, the third pivotal event in the negotiations. The Security Council meeting was a tremendous boost to Panama's already great commitment. It not only added to Panama's commitment the commitment of others, but also brought the power of principle to bear on Panama's position. Moreover, it took place in a context of perceived American weakness and unwillingness to participate in foreign interventions (i.e., a context of diminished U.S. control over outcomes).

Once again, the issue power balance was altered in Panama's favor. The United States was again forced to determine its objectives: unilateral control or secure control. By choosing the latter objective, the United States committed itself to negotiations with Panama, for it now recognized that secure control could come about only with Panamanian consent.

Less than twelve months later, the United States and Panama had agreed on a formula (the Kissinger-Tack principles). Although domestic events in both countries slowed the progress over the next two and one-half years, the election of President Carter led to a new sense of commitment to negotiation on the part of the United States, and a relatively brief detail phase.

One of the most striking observations about the Panama Canal negotiations is that it was Panama that consistently took the tactical initiative, from the 1964 riots to Torrijos's eleventh-hour demand for large financial rewards. The reasons are clear. Panama was trying to get as much as possible from the United States, whereas the U.S. was trying to preserve as much as possible. The Canal negotiations were a classic example of what Iklé termed "redistribution" negotiations, in which one side seeks major changes in its favor.[95] Decolonization negotiations, which the Canal negotiations closely resembled, generally are redistributive in nature.

Panama's objective was to persuade the United States to accept that it could preserve very little of the old treaty. For the most part, Panama succeeded. At the beginning of 1964, the United States enjoyed unilateral control over Canal operations, administration, and defense; effective, if not legal, sovereignty over the Canal Zone; and a treaty that was to be in force "in perpetuity." With the 1977 agreement, Panama had gained the promise of eventual unilateral control over administration and operation, shared control over defense, recognition of Panamanian sovereignty in the Canal Zone, and a treaty with an expiration date.

Panama's success was the result of its efforts over thirteen years at altering the issue power balance in its favor. In 1964, the United States had more alternatives and greater control than Panama and commitment to its position almost equal to Panama. Panama directed its tactics to shifting the issue power balance by decreasing American alternatives, commitment, and control while increasing its own.

Panama's warnings/threats centered on the possibility of insurrection, sabotage, or disruption in the Canal Zone, in short, actions that would significantly raise the costs of American control and of American commitment to its preferred outcome. The 1964 riots brought the reality of this possibility to the Americans' attention. From then on, Panamanian warnings and threats possessed credibility, not only to the Americans, but to the Panamanians themselves, who perhaps needed the 1964 riots to convince themselves that their degree of control over outcomes was greater than they had thought.

Over the next thirteen years, Panama's leaders, and especially Torrijos, periodically used warnings and threats to enhance their issue power position. The warnings and threats were used at times when it appeared the United States was backtracking or losing interest in a negotiated solution. Torrijos's threatening rhetoric in the fall of 1971 followed Nixon's earlier proposal of a formula that would have undone, in Panamanian eyes, much of the progress the countries had made. Similarly, during the American presidential campaign in 1976, Torrijos again used threatening rhetoric to try to prevent the United States from hardening its position.

Torrijos skillfully walked a thin line. His threats were subtle, and seldom explicit; his warnings often more akin to pleadings. This was wise behavior, given that the United States had considerably greater structural power. An attempt to actualize a threat could have increased both U.S. commitment and willingness to exercise its potential (i.e., structurally based) ability to control outcomes unilaterally. The use of warnings and threats was indeed Panama's most effective tactic. In a redistribution negotiation, the side demanding major changes can offer very little except a lack of trouble.

A number of American officials later revealed how seriously they regarded the threat of violence. Secretary of Defense Harold Brown, testifying before Congress in 1978, asked: "What do we want? Do we want a situation where we may have to use force over and over and over again in order to preserve the operability of the Canal or do we want a situation where the people of Panama see themselves as correctly having an important stake in keeping the Canal operating?"[96] General D. P. McAuliffe, commander of U.S. forces in the Canal Zone, asserted that defense of the Canal against a guerrilla or terrorist threat supported by a hostile Panamanian populace and government would require an open-ended commitment of between 40,000 and 100,000 U.S. ground troops.[97]

Panama effectively used coalition building. The Kissinger-Tack principles were signed within a year of the Security Council meeting in Panama City; the link between the two events is undeniable. In the ensuing years, Torrijos used coalition building to bolster Panama's alternatives and its commitment. His meetings with Castro and other left-wing leaders, in particular, opened new alternatives by demonstrating that Panama need not remain an ally of the United States. His meetings with other Latin American and Third World leaders bolstered Panama's commitment by joining to it the commitment of other sympathetic states.

Whereas Panama used the tactic of warnings and threats in desperation to stop U.S. backtracking and revive waning American attention, it used the tactic of coalition building when it needed to push the negotiations forward. Thus, Panama tended to alternate between the two tactics depending upon its perception of the state of the negotiation process.

Panama's tactics were most effective in determining the nature of the formula (the Kissinger-Tack accord). Formulas deal with principles, notions of justice, and a general definition of what the outcome should look like. The formula sets the boundaries within which the details are to be negotiated. It is thus greatly affected by changes in the issue power balance, since that balance describes the nature of the actors' interdependent relationship over the particular issue in question. Formulas reflect the issue power balance; they reflect each side's perception of the balance of alternatives, commitment, and control.

Details are negotiated within the framework set out by the formula. But within these bounds, the negotiations are more likely to be guided by the structural power balance than by behavioral power. For details deal with quantifiable factors: sums of money, numbers of bases, years of duration, and so on. In the Canal negotiations, the American structural power advantage was evidenced in the detail stage. The United States dangled offers of financial reward before the economically beleaguered Panamanians; it warned that the number of protreaty votes in the Senate was dwindling and firmly demanded increased defense rights while Torrijos twisted in the wind of impending economic collapse. In effect, during the detail stage the United States was saying: "You've got your formula, which recognizes those principles and rights you have been fighting for, but now we want to ensure that, within the bounds of the formula, we retain as much as possible of what we had before." And this the United States did. It gave sovereignty, but retained defense rights; it retained perpetuity (at least in terms of defense rights), while conceding the term; it promised financial remuneration, while ensuring that the bulk of this came from Canal tolls, not from the U.S. Treasury.

Contextual Factors

The majority of Panamanians disliked the original Canal treaty from the time it was signed in 1903, but it was not until 1964 that they began actively to push for a new treaty. This fact underscores the critical role contextual factors played in the negotiations.

No event in international relations can be analyzed in isolation from the historical context in which it occurs. The 1964 riots occurred in an era of worldwide decolonization and the American civil rights movement. Had the riots occurred in earlier decades, when American military intervention in Latin America was the norm, they probably would have been quickly squelched. They certainly would not have launched a negotiation process.

The Kissinger-Tack formula was negotiated within the context of post-Vietnam U.S. foreign policy, the sudden dramatic appearance of powerful Third World producer cartels, and an easing in East-West tensions.[98] This milieu made Panama's tactics, particularly the tactic of coalition building, all the more effective in weakening U.S. commitment and bolstering Panama's. Torrijos clearly understood the significance of historical context and used it to Panama's advantage throughout the formula phase of the negotiations.

The detail phase, on the other hand, took place in the context of a nascent resurgence of a hard-line U.S. foreign policy. Although President Carter looked favorably upon a new treaty, many in Congress were determined to block an agreement. An American participant in the negotiations described how the context had begun to change by 1977: "The treaties slipped through a window of time when cold war views were coming back. . . . [The treaties] went in with just barely a moment to spare. You couldn't have done it a year later."[99]

If it is true that people make history, an important aspect of context is the personality factor. Until Torrijos came to power, Panama suffered from internal political uncertainties and a lack of consensus. Under Torrijos's essentially one-man rule, Panama gained a new sense of assertiveness and unity of purpose. Moreover, Torrijos was a remarkably effective tactician.

The United States, on the other hand, experienced the trauma of military defeat, the resignation of a president, and a heated political campaign. It was not until Jimmy Carter's election brought a brief period of political tranquillity that the United States could move forward in what had been stalemated negotiations. To Panama's advantage, Carter brought to this tranquillity a more liberal foreign policy.

FIVE

U.S.–Spanish Bases Negotiations

The catalyst for the Panama Canal negotiations was the crisis caused by the 1964 riots in the Canal Zone and Panama City. Similarly, British-Icelandic negotiations during the Cod Wars were the result of the crises caused by the confrontation between Icelandic and British ships in the North Atlantic. Many negotiations follow such crises, which are often provoked by one of the parties (usually the structurally weaker one) so as to bring about a negotiated solution. The U.S.–Spanish bases negotiations, however, followed not a crisis between the two sides but rather a gradual convergence of the two toward an interdependent relationship.

In the immediate postwar period, there was virtually no possibility of an interdependent relationship developing between the United States and Spain over any issue. The United States and its European allies were understandably bitter toward the Franco regime. Although never actually entering World War II, Franco Spain had left little doubt as to which side it favored. Following the war, the Western allies adopted a policy of aggressive political ostracism of Spain, including public calls for the overthrow of the Franco regime.[1] In the face of this ostracism, Spain retreated behind walls of isolationism and paranoia. Franco preached his country's neutralism and sovereignty and scoffed at the West Europeans who, he claimed, had subordinated their national wills to the United States.

DEVELOPING AN INTERDEPENDENT RELATIONSHIP

The Diagnostic Phase

In the late 1940s and early 1950s, however, the United States and Spain found themselves unilaterally converging toward an interdependent relationship. The catalyst for this convergence was the outbreak of the Cold War. Almost overnight, military strategy began to supplant all other factors as the guiding light of American foreign policy. As Stalin's stock fell, Franco's could not help but rise.

In October 1947, the U.S. Department of State's Policy Planning Staff, under the direction of George Kennan, prepared a study calling for normalization in U.S.–Spanish relations.[2] Its argument was based on the belief that the policy of ostracism was not working (i.e., had not led to the overthrow of Franco) and that Spain could play a useful role in Western defense. Although the policy paper had minimal immediate impact—the Truman White House still strongly opposed dealing with the Franco regime—it nevertheless gave evidence of the new position toward Spain gaining ground among midlevel policy makers.

The strongest backing for a new policy toward Spain came from the Pentagon. The military's interest in Spain was based primarily on geo-strategic considerations: Spain was farther from Eastern Europe than any NATO country except Portugal; it overlooked the shipping lanes of the western Mediterranean and eastern Atlantic; and it offered the West a natural fallback position behind the Pyrenees.[3] The navy was the center of pro-Spain sentiment in the Pentagon; Admiral Forrest Sherman, chief of Naval Operations, was particularly eager to gain access to additional Mediterranean ports.

Spain also enjoyed growing support in Congress, especially among Catholic, extreme anti-Communist, and prodefense members. Senator Harry Cain of Washington, a member of the prodefense group, described Spain as "a huge airfield of 195,000 square miles."[4] Combined with military leaders and certain commercial interests, the pro-Spain coalition in Congress became known as the "Spanish lobby." This lobby was assisted by a Washington lawyer on Franco's payroll, and by José Felix de Lequerica, Spanish ambassador-at-large, who made frequent visits to Washington in the late 1940s.

But perhaps the most important factors in bringing about a sea change in U.S. policy toward Spain were two contextual events: the fall of China in 1949 and the outbreak of the Korean War in 1950. The fall of China presented the specter of a monolithic Communist empire stretching from the Baltic to the Pacific. Truman's aversion to dealing with Franco was suddenly overshadowed by the perceived need to bolster the Western alliance. In the fall of 1949, Admiral Richard L. Conolly, commander of the U.S. naval forces in the eastern Atlantic and western Mediterranean, successfully persuaded the White House to allow an official navy visit to a Spanish Mediterranean port.[5]

The outbreak of the Korean War in 1950 only confirmed the changed perceptions brought about by the fall of China. At the time most policy makers felt the Korean War was a feint, intended to distract the West while Moscow prepared a European invasion. A closer relationship with Spain was thus all the more enticing. The Korean War seemed also to confirm the conclusions reached in the important National Security Council interdepartmental study, NSC-68, completed earlier in 1950. The authors of NSC-68 argued that the United States needed to increase its military commitment greatly if it was to meet the Soviet threat successfully. Implicit in its recommendations was the need for a network of overseas bases.[6]

In the face of what was perceived as a threatening world situation, the Joint Chiefs of Staff, in May 1950, issued an urgent memorandum: "[We] strongly recommend that the Department of State take action without delay to assure to the United States and its allies military accessibility to and military cooperation with Spain."[7]

At first, President Truman refused to allow the growing fear of the Soviet Union to alter his policy toward Spain. The State Department also remained opposed to a closer relationship with Franco. In response to the Joint Chiefs' memorandum, the State Department replied that it found their recommendation "politically impractical."[8] But after the outbreak of the Korean War, the tide of anti-Sovietism became too strong for even Truman's democratic principles to withstand. On June 8, 1951, Truman endorsed another NSC policy paper which recommended that the United States establish military bases in Spain.[9]

Similarly, Spain found itself converging toward a relationship with the United States. Although Franco received popular support for his isolationist policy, particularly from such influential and important groups as the Catholic Church (which strongly opposed close contact with "Protestant" America) and the military (which feared loss of identity and power if forced to join an alliance), certain factors were working to modify his position. For one, although Spain was never involved in combat in World War II, its economy was in worse shape than most other European states. Still suffering the ravages of the Civil War, denied Marshall Plan aid by the United States and access to markets by most of the world, Spain was finding its isolationism and ostracism difficult to bear. The glaring contrast between the rapid economic growth of the Marshall Plan European economies and the stagnation of the Spanish economy was all too obvious to Franco.

The seeming rise in Soviet power and ambitions also modified Spain's position. Anticommunism, after all, was a fundamental tenet of Francoism. Soviet domination of Eastern Europe, combined with the Chinese Revolution and the Korean War, led to a change in Spain's professed nonalignment and neutrality.

The result of this mutual convergence was the development of an interdependent relationship between the United States and Spain. Specifically, the United States wanted the use of military bases on Spanish soil, and Spain wanted American economic aid and Western acceptance of the Franco regime. Growing recognition of this new interdependent relationship resulted in an exchange of ambassadors in 1950, the commencement of informal negotiations in 1951, and of formal negotiations in 1952.

The Prenegotiation Issue Power Balance

The United States entered the negotiations with an issue power advantage. It possessed more alternatives than Spain for achieving its desired outcome. Spain was not the only nation bordering the Mediterranean; the United States had the option of using bases in a number of other countries, including Portugal, Morocco, Libya, Italy, and Greece. Spain, on the other hand, had no alternatives to the United States for economic and military aid. Furthermore, fulfillment of Spain's desire for acceptance would be truly meaningful only if it came from the United States, the undisputed leader of the Western world.

Although both sides desired an agreement, Spain appears to have had greater commitment. A closer relationship with the United States was critically important to Spain's entire economy, as well as being militarily important. The stakes were thus higher for Franco; he had more to gain in an agreement than did the United States, and more to lose if no agreement were reached. Such a situation is not surprising given the tremendous disparity in structural power between the United States and Spain. Spain could provide the United States nothing irreplaceable or even crucially important.

Commitment, as defined in chapter 2, is a two-edged sword. In this instance, greater commitment was a source of issue power weakness for Spain. Spain's commitment was to achieving something that did not already exist, a close relationship with the United States, with all the benefits that entailed. Its commitment was based as much on need as desire. (Spain's position may be usefully contrasted with that of Panama during the Canal negotiations. Panama also had a greater commitment than did the United States. But Panama's commitment was to overcoming an undesirable situation—continued American control of the Canal. It was based more on aspiration than need, and thus served as a source of issue power strength.)

U.S. commitment to its preferred outcome was also strong. As will be seen below, the United States preferred a much less formal and wide-ranging agreement than Spain desired. This preference was the result of the powerful constraints on closer U.S.–Spanish relations deriving from anti-Franco sentiment in both Congress and among NATO allies. The extreme caution with which the United States proceeded in the early stages of the negotiations is indicative of these constraints. More-oever, because the United States had more alternatives, thus making Spanish bases less important in America's overall strategic calculus, Franco would find it difficult to weaken American commitment to its minimalist preferred outcome, or to increase American commitment to Spain's preferred outcome.

The final criterion of issue power, control, was not a relevant factor in the negotiations. Control was defined as the ability to achieve desired outcomes unilaterally (see chapter 2), which neither side could do in this case. Though the United States did possess enough military power conceivably to take Spanish territory by force, this is hardly an ideal way to establish overseas bases. Similarly, Spain could not unilaterally acquire the economic and military aid it wanted from the United States. (Again, a comparison with the Panama Canal negotiations is instruc-tive. In that case, the United States, because it maintained military forces in the Canal Zone, administered the Zone and could probably defeat a Panamanian effort to change the situation; it had the advantage of control, at least initially.)

Thus, the United States possessed an advantage in issue power when talks began in 1952. Spain's tactics throughout the negotiations aimed at closing this issue power gap and thus its dependence on the United States. Specifically, Spain's tactics emphasized (1) increasing American commitment to an outcome favorable to Spain, (2) trying to make it *appear* that Spain's commitment was not really that great, and (3) con-vincing the United States that it did not have so many alternatives as it thought and that, in any case, Spain was a better choice than the other alternatives.

THE 1951–1953 NEGOTIATIONS

The Search for a Formula

The Americans' primary objective in the negotiations was to secure additional overseas bases. From the American point of view, the ideal way to gain access to bases in Spain was to "rent" them, that is, to pay the Spanish government an annual fee for the right to use bases on Spanish soil. By renting the bases, the United States hoped to avoid a close alliance with Spain. The desire to keep Franco at arm's length derived from two sources. First, a tremendous undercurrent of ani-mosity toward the Franco regime remained in the United States. It was felt not only by the Truman administration, but also by a majority in Congress. Second, the United States was sensitive to the sentiments of its allies in the new NATO alliance. The British and French, in particular, never hesitated to express their disapproval of closer American ties to Franco (not only because of aversion to Franco, but also because of a fear that if Spain joined the West's defense system the Pyrenees, and not the Rhine, would become the line of defense). The United States wished to ensure that its dealings with Spain did not become a source of NATO dissension. Therefore, the United States was initially not anxious to provide Spain with extensive economic or military aid, and preferred to regard the upcoming bases negotiations as one between landlord and tenant.

To Spain, the negotiations represented an opportunity to end its political ostracism, to gain a greater degree of international acceptance as well as substantial economic and military aid. In any event, Spain rejected the American concept of leasing the bases; instead, Franco wanted to share the bases, implying close political and military cooperation.

The initial objectives of the two sides revealed an important issue which was to reappear throughout the search for a formula. This issue centered on the question of what exactly was being negotiated. The United States was negotiating for a tangible asset: the use of military facilities. Spain, however, was primarily negotiating for an intangible asset: international respectability. Admittedly, international respectability had its tangible side (military and economic aid). But it became increasingly apparent throughout the negotiations that the intangible objective of international respectability and acceptance by the West was the paramount goal of the Franco regime.

The search for a formula began soon after ambassadors were exchanged in early 1951. Truman sent Admiral Forrest Sherman to Madrid to meet with Franco to try to determine whether an agreement was possible. When Sherman asked Franco the price for American use of several naval and air bases, Franco reportedly requested nearly one billion dollars in economic and military aid.[10] He also wanted a bilateral defense pact with the United States, if not membership in NATO.

But as already noted, one of the Americans' most important objectives was to prevent an agreement with Spain from damaging the cohesion of the Atlantic alliance, whose European members, especially France and Britain, were opposed to the Franco regime. Secretary of State Dean Acheson expressed American concerns about alliance cohesion several months after preliminary talks began in early 1951. He said the United States would not offer military aid to Spain without the consent of its European allies.[11] The United States clearly valued alliance cohesion over bases in Spain.

Franco realized that America's strong commitment to its European allies could weaken its commitment to reaching an agreement with

Spain. He responded with two tactics: one a concession, to remove the linkage between Spanish bases and alliance sentiment; the other a warning, to increase American commitment to an agreement with Spain.

Several times throughout the spring and summer of 1951, Franco's government issued statements to the effect that Spain was not interested in joining NATO and did not want to interfere in NATO affairs.[12] This position was a concession, for Franco was indicating that Spain was willing to be treated as a second-class ally of the United States. Another Spanish concession was more symbolic than significant, but revealed nonetheless Franco's concern that British and French hostility might diminish U.S. commitment. In July 1951, Franco announced a reshuffling of his cabinet which noticeably deemphasized Falange party representation.

Franco combined these concessionary moves with warnings intended to increase U.S. commitment to an agreement. He did so by repeatedly emphasizing the instability of the French government and noting with dramatic alarm the growing power of the French Communists.[13] Franco accused the British Labour party of being pacifist and unlikely to support the United States in a conflict with the Soviet Union.

These warnings were directed not only at American commitment, but also at America's perceived alternatives. Franco was trying to communicate that Spain would be a more loyal supporter of U.S. policy than would France and Britain.

As the preliminary talks continued, it became obvious that the Pentagon was the primary force in favor of U.S. bases in Spain. Indeed, in July 1951, President Truman publicly stated that U.S. policy in negotiations with Spain would be based on the advice of the Pentagon.[14] For obvious reasons, Franco sought to promote and encourage the Pentagon's position, since to do so would increase U.S. commitment to reaching an agreement. The more acutely the United States felt the need for overseas bases, the less committed it would be to its minimalist preferred outcome, and the more likely Spain would be to achieve a favorable agreement.

Franco thus encouraged the United States to see Spain as a potential bulwark against Soviet activity in the Mediterranean and North Africa. He repeatedly asserted his deep-rooted anticommunism, and the state-controlled Spanish press constantly referred to the growing Soviet threat. In January 1951, just before the commencement of formal negotiations, Franco made it known that Spanish troops could be used wherever they were needed to fight communism.[15]

Throughout this preliminary stage, the Americans essentially allowed Franco to make all the moves. The only definitive position the

United States took was to proceed with formal negotiations in 1952. Yet Franco must have been emboldened by his own rhetoric and tactics, so much so that by early 1952 he was making specific demands and actually outlining a proposed treaty. On January 25, his minister of the army, General Augustin Muñoz Grandes, presented an extensive list of Spain's wants in return for American use of naval and air bases. The list included hundreds of millions of dollars' worth of military equipment, as well as huge sums of general economic aid.[16]

The American response was not enthusiastic. Secretary Acheson suggested at a news conference in March that the United States envisaged an agreement along the lines of $100 million in economic aid in return for "standby" use of military bases.[17] Franco had miscalculated. He mistook America's relative silence throughout 1951 to mean that the issue balance had shifted, and that the United States was equally committed to reaching a quick, and, for Spain, lucrative, agreement. Indeed, Franco's tactics had increased U.S. interest; the Americans did, after all, agree to transform the preliminary talks of 1951 into formal negotiations. But Washington was still constrained by the NATO factor. Moreover, the United States possessed enough alternatives so that it did not feel Franco's price was reasonable.

Acheson's remarks led to a stalemate. Spain was clearly angered by the meager U.S. economic offer of only $100 million, and by the "landlord-tenant" agreement the United States still envisioned. Negotiations were suspended for a month, ostensibly pending the arrival of a new American ambassador.

Franco now was on the defensive. He had successfully persuaded the Americans into proceeding with negotiations, but had not been successful in bringing about the type of formula he wanted. Franco needed to alter the issue power balance even more if he hoped to achieve his goals of a close bilateral military relationship and large sums of financial aid.

As a new round of negotiations began in the spring of 1952, Franco adopted a strategy of mixing tough tactics with soft ones. The Spanish press launched a series of commentaries, ostensibly aimed at the domestic audience, which assured the people of Spain that the country's military bases would never be ceded and that Spain's sovereign rights would never be given up.[18] The series was a warning to the United States that negotiations would be endangered if the Americans continued to insist on their landlord-tenant formula.

This stern communication was coupled with a softer tactic which bordered on pleading. On April 15, Franco held a highly publicized meeting with General Antonio de Oliveira Salazar of Portugal. In a joint communiqué, the two leaders pledged commitment to the defense of the West against Soviet aggression. Franco went on to say that Spain deserved the same treatment from the United States as Portugal received.[19] The message was clear. Portugal, which shared Spain's authoritarian form of government, had not only been invited to join NATO, but was also the recipient of extensive American aid. Why could similar close ties not be forged between the United States and Spain?

The United States responded to these tactics in the same manner as it had to the earlier Spanish tactics; it essentially ignored them. In response to Franco's warning, the United States neither conceded on its landlord-tenant proposal nor abandoned the negotiations. This approach amounted to calling Franco's bluff; either he accept the landlord-tenant proposal, with its modest rent, or he abandon the negotiations. American commitment to its preferred outcome remained strong.

By the summer of 1952, Spain must have felt overwhelming frustration. None of its tactics—concessions, warnings, pleadings—had succeeded in increasing American commitment to an agreement favorable to Spain. But Franco could try one more tactic, one that would test American intentions once and for all: the threat to end the negotiations.

In July 1952, Franco delivered a memorandum to the American negotiators in which he termed the U.S. financial offer "completely inadequate," presented a shopping list of military equipment worth nearly $1.5 billion, and insisted that a "fundamental [defense] agreement" must be a part of any package.[20] Furthermore, Franco threatened to walk out of the negotiations unless the United States agreed to these demands, to a bilateral defense pact, and Spanish inclusion in the Mutual Security Aid Act for Europe.[21] A threat is effective only if backed by a strong and credible commitment to carry it out if necessary. During the next several months Spain expressed this commitment by launching a bitter public campaign against the United States, not only for its stubborn position in the negotiations, but also for such unrelated "crimes" as the continued "colonization" of Puerto Rico.[22] This protracted tirade served to prepare the Spanish public for a possible break in negotiations, and thus served to enhance the credibility of Franco's threat. But the ultimate objective was to test U.S. intentions by threatening to leave the United States completely empty-handed.

The United States was now forced to make a response. Having already conceded to a great extent on its concern for British and French sensitivities by proceeding with formal negotiations, the United States had to determine how to reconcile what was left of those concerns with the type of close relationship Franco was demanding.

Faced with an impending walkout by Spain, and yet unwilling to agree to Franco's formula of bases in exchange for close ties and extensive aid, the United States offered a new formula. Specifically, the United States promised that, though it could not at this time offer a mutual defense agreement or provide Spain with more than limited economic aid, a bases agreement between the two countries—even if under a "landlord-tenant" formula—would mark the beginning of closer bilateral ties. Clearly implied was the promise of greater economic aid and closer military ties in the future: "While no assurance regarding future aid can be given to any country, our good faith can be judged by the experience of other countries who have participated in cooperative projects with the U.S." The United States also pointed out that, though the first priority for U.S. military aid had to go to the frontline NATO states, it indirectly contributed to Spain's security.[23] Within two weeks the Spanish press had ceased its angry criticism of the United States, and by December 1952, Franco was lauding the "identity of views" Spain shared with the United States.

The very fact that the United States made this promise—a significant qualitative difference from its earlier position—revealed that American commitment to its preferred outcome, an arms-length relationship with Spain, had weakened sufficiently so that the prospect of reaching no agreement was rendered unacceptable. But the United States was still far from accepting Spain's preferred outcome.

There now existed a formula acceptable to both sides, specifically, American use of bases in exchange for rent payments now and the promise of greater rewards in the future. This formula was considerably closer to the original American conception, however, than it was to Spain's.

After the preliminary talks in 1951, Spain had felt sufficiently confident to demand significant economic aid and close military ties. What it ended up with was a formula based on the promise of unspecified future rewards. The American issue power advantage was so great that Spain really had very little chance of gaining a more favorable formula. Not until Spain played its ultimate card, the threat to veto the negotiations, did the United States depart from its original position. That Spain accepted this formula so readily speaks to Franco's recognition that his issue power position was weak and unlikely to be strengthened in the foreseeable future.

The Detail Phase and the Outcome

The detail phase was relatively brief and uneventful; it was devoid of the heated activity that characterized the search for a formula. On September 25, 1953, the two sides reached agreement on three distinct, but linked, texts: on economic aid, on defense, and on defense assistance. In exchange for the use of air bases at Zaragoza, Torrejon, and Moron and a naval base at Rota, the United States agreed to provide Madrid with $85 million in economic aid and $141 million in military aid over the next year, with an additional $350 million in military aid to be provided by 1957.[24] These terms were a far cry from the nearly $1 billion Franco had originally desired but also were better than the original American offer. Although the agreement made the two countries tacit military partners, it did not specify the mutual military obligations of the two governments in the event of war; it was thus not the formal mutual defense treaty Franco wanted.

Nevertheless, Spain gained three important things in the agreement. First, despite the absence of a formal alliance with the United States, the very presence of American forces on Spanish soil and American aid in Spanish coffers amounted to a substantial degree of international acceptance of the Franco regime. This had been one of Franco's major though intangible objectives throughout the negotiations. Second, Franco had gained from the United States the all-important promise of future concessions. He had little choice but to take this promise at face value, since the alternative would have meant a break in the negotiations. The third, and perhaps most important, thing Spain gained from the agreement was a solidifying of the new relationship with the United States. As a result, once the bases were operational, the United States would have a growing stake in keeping them operational. In other words, the more the United States came to rely on its bases in Spain, the greater would be American dependence on Spain, and thus the greater would be Spain's issue power in future base rights negotiations.

The 1953 agreement was to last for ten years. In 1963, it was renewed for five years with only limited modifications. Despite predictions to the contrary, Franco did not push for Spanish membership in NATO in the 1963 renewal talks. Opposition to Spanish membership, now coming primarily from Scandinavian members of NATO, remained strong, and Franco evidently did not feel the time was ripe to attempt to negotiate for a revised formula. Both sides seemed to realize that if "either side pushed too hard, the American-Spanish connection might have severed just when it was beginning to produce its fruit."[25]

Spain did succeed, however, in slightly enhancing its ties with the United States. The two countries agreed to establish a Joint Consultative Committee on Defense Matters in Madrid, which would meet monthly to discuss matters of mutual concern and to improve military cooperation. The United States also offered to provide Spain with an additional $100 million in military assistance and $100 million in Export-Import Bank loans, and Spain agreed to purchase 50 million dollars' worth of U.S. arms in an offset arrangement.[26]

Essentially, however, the 1963 renewal agreement kept intact the formula of 1953—bases in exchange for limited financial assistance, but without formal military and defense ties.

Communicating Tactics

Spain's initial tactical objective in the negotiations leading to the 1953 agreement was to persuade the United States to take a greater interest in Spanish bases. Particular tactics included domestic political concessions to weaken anti-Spain sentiment, warnings of French and British instability designed to make Spain look more appealing, and an attempt to form a coalition with Portugal's Salazar. But these tactics were pursued outside the negotiation process, for the negotiations were not about Spain's domestic politics, or British and French political stability, or Portuguese-U.S. relations. Spain had to communicate these tactics indirectly.

Unfortunately for Franco, his domestic political concessions were not credible and thus not persuasive because the message they were intended to communicate, that Spain was becoming more democratic, was not believable. A minor cabinet reshuffle was insignificant and transparent. Moreover, Franco took no steps to broaden civil liberties, recognize opposition groups, or loosen his personal hold over the Spanish government. In short, neither the United States nor its European allies were persuaded that the Franco regime was changing.

Franco's warnings of political instability in Britain and France also lacked credibility, since there were no signs that British or French withdrawal from the Western alliance was imminent. The British and French loathing of Franco and his regime further diminished the objectivity and impact of his warnings.

Franco's attempt at forming a coalition with Portugal's Salazar was not credible because Portugal had little influence over the United States. In any event, Salazar was unwilling to place at risk his own positive relationship with the United States to help Franco.

For these reasons, Spain's tactics failed to change the American perception of Spain's importance or of the Franco regime's attractiveness. The result was an American tactic of aloofness and stalling, a tactic largely the product of the powerful constraints on U.S. policy. A tactic of aloofness and stalling is communicated by inaction: refusing to respond to the opponent's tactics, making few or no concessions, and generally treating the negotiations as a low priority.

One would think that this type of tactic is easy to make credible, since inaction speaks for itself. But Franco had difficulty understanding the American tactic of aloofness, and he was certainly not persuaded to limit his demands. To the contrary, his demands and expectations continued to rise. Franco apparently mistook American inaction for acquiescence.

The implication is that a tactic of aloofness, which by definition is passively communicated, is not always understood by the opponent. And if it is not understood, it cannot be persuasive.

Franco eventually realized that the American policy of aloofness reflected lack of interest, not acquiescence, and that his tactics had failed to persuade the United States. This realization led him to adopt the tactic of threatening to end the negotiations.

He communicated this threat directly and unequivocally, not only to the U.S. negotiators, but to the Spanish public as well. This move endowed his threat with great credibility. He was painting himself into a corner with both the Americans and his own people. Only the U.S. response could free him from actually carrying out his threat.

Franco's threat succeeded in altering the Americans' perception of the problem by forcing them to see that an agreement on Spanish bases would require more from the United States than a nominal rent payment. Furthermore, the Spanish threat persuaded the United States to see that the negotiations concerned more than merely bases and dollars. They also concerned Spain's acceptance by the West. The U.S. response to the Spanish threat reflected this concern; the American promise was of closer ties in the future, not of more money. Thus, Spain's threat to end the negotiations changed both the U.S. perception of what the negotiations were about as well as U.S. behavior in the negotiation process.

THE 1968–1970 NEGOTIATIONS

The Search for a New Formula

As the 1968 renewal deadline approached, Spain returned to the offensive. Franco's objective was to replace the landlord–tenant formula with a closer bilateral relationship. By 1968, the United States had enjoyed Spanish bases for fifteen years. These bases had become an integral part of the American defense system. Moreover, it was now over twenty years since the end of World War II, twenty years during which Spain had proved its loyalty to the Western cause.

Spain thus felt it deserved more. The 1953 formula had made Spain a second-class ally of the United States. As a Spanish official put it: "The West gives us a little, takes what we have to offer, and on top of that makes us use the delivery entrance."[27]

Moreover, many Spaniards had begun to feel that the American bases placed Spain at considerable risk in the event of a U.S.-Soviet confrontation, since the bases would almost certainly be prime Soviet targets. This concern was heightened in January 1966, when a U.S. B-52 bomber accidentally released four unarmed hydrogen bombs, three of which landed near the Spanish fishing village of Palomares. Although an isolated incident, it received extensive coverage in the controlled Spanish press, and added ammunition to Franco's argument for the need of a new formula, one that would put Spain on an equal footing with America's other allies.

Franco began the 1968 negotiations with extensive demands. Specifically, Spain requested that the existing agreement, which was in the form of an executive agreement, be replaced with a formal mutual defense treaty; that the United States make renewed efforts to have Spain admitted into NATO; and that the United States provide $1.2 billion in military aid and equipment.

The United States responded by offering a joint declaration on defense, but not a full-fledged alliance; a marginal increase in cooperation between NATO and Spanish forces; and $100 million in military aid, $100 million in arms on credit, and $100 million in Export-Import Bank loans.[28]

The United States had wanted to renew the 1963 agreement without substantial changes; in other words, to retain the original formula. American commitment to obtaining bases in Spain, instead of growing over the previous fifteen years, showed signs of waning. The development of nuclear submarines and intercontinental missiles had increased American alternatives, since they reduced the need for an extensive overseas base system. Nuclear submarines could be based on the U.S. East Coast at only slightly greater expense. The war in Vietnam was also beginning to affect U.S. policy, with Congress now increasingly wary of foreign involvement of any kind. In the words of Secretary of State Dean Rusk, the time had come for the United States to "reduce its profile overseas."[29] In fact, if anything, American commitment was lower than ever before. Government sources were leaking reports that the Pentagon regarded Spanish bases as "important, but not vital."[30]

Spain's commitment, on the other hand, remained high. Franco was eager to win greater American aid, since Spain's economy still lagged behind most of the rest of Europe. Franco's desire to join the Western defense system also remained high. As the United States continued to be Spain's only alternative for achieving either of these goals, the issue power balance remained favorable to the United States.

By September 28, the day on which the 1963 agreement was to expire, it was obvious that more time would be needed. Spain had reduced its $1.2 billion aid request to a "rock bottom" $700 million, plus a mutual defense agreement.[31] But the United States did not budge. The Spanish delegation was called home, and the negotiations officially ended.

Under the terms of the 1963 agreement, a six-month grace period was allowed before the agreement was formally terminated. It gave Franco until March 1969 to consider new tactics to increase U.S. commitment.

The tactics Franco initially adopted were similar to those he had used in the earlier negotiations, combining hard- and soft-line tactics. The soft line became evident in November, when Spain reduced its asking price to $400 million.[32] The hard line came in the form of a veiled warning Spanish Foreign Minister Fernando Castiella made to West German Chancellor Kurt Kiesinger. Castiella told Kiesinger that Spain would have to consider a neutralist course if the West was not more forthcoming. Spain would take this action "without pleasure, but with dignity," Castiella said.[33] Franco was once again testing the limits of American commitment.

The United States responded, but not by raising its financial offer. Rather, Washington announced a series of official visits to Spain, beginning with a trip by Secretary Rusk in late November. The purpose of this gesture was to counter the Spanish warning by signaling that the West, or at least the United States, did not take Spain for granted. The visits may also have served the purpose of making it easier politically for Franco to reduce his financial demands even more. But the overall message was nevertheless ambiguous. Spanish bases were important enough to warrant high-level visits, but not a formal defense commitment or a substantial increase in rent payments.

As the new deadline—March 26, 1969—approached, Spain became increasingly worried. Franco had hoped that his walkout in September, combined with the inauguration of the more conservative Nixon administration, would increase U.S. commitment. Indeed, a February 1969 National Security Council report determined that the bases in Spain remained "of great importance to the United States."[34] But America's issue power advantage was so great that U.S. negotiators could stick to their hard-line offer.

Moreover, a rift had occurred within the Spanish leadership. Foreign Minister Castiella's position had begun to deteriorate. His tactic of quietly threatening a policy of neutrality if Spain's demands were not met was strongly opposed by the Spanish military, who feared that the United States might call Castiella's bluff.[35] The United States discovered this internal schism when Spanish military officers involved in the negotiations complained to their American counterparts. It was a boon to the United States, for it revealed the intensity of Spain's desire, or, at least, the desire of Spain's military, which usually succeeded in capturing Franco's ear. The warning of possible neutrality had thus backfired; the result was an even stronger American issue power advantage.

Several days before the March 26 deadline, Spain reduced its aid request even further, to $300 million, and dropped demands for a formal defense pact.[36] The United States improved its offer slightly, to $175 million, but made no other concessions. The only thing the two sides agreed on was yet another extension of the negotiation deadline. In the words of one analyst, "the parties found themselves in a chicken dilemma where the only escape lay in an alteration of the parameters of the bargaining relationship."[37]

In other words, the two sides needed a new formula. Spain had never been happy with the original landlord-tenant formula, but had accepted it because its weak issue power position gave it no alternative. Franco felt that if he could not get the formula he wanted, he should get as much as possible out of the formula offered him; hence, his large aid (rent) requests. But the United States was in such a strong position that it did not feel the need to make serious concessions on either defense guarantees or aid. In fact, the United States had come close to adopting a "take it or leave it" attitude. Sources in the Pentagon claimed that the primary argument for keeping the bases in Spain was that it would be more costly to dismantle them.[38]

The Spanish were in a dilemma. Acceptance of the meager American offer would reveal all too clearly how much they needed and wanted an agreement. Not only might that hurt Franco's position domestically, but it also would place Spain in a weaker position in any subsequent renewal negotiations. On the other hand, if Franco did not accept the American offer, the negotiations would probably come to an end. The solution was to find a new formula that would be acceptable to the Americans but would also allow Spain to save face while agreeing to the American aid terms.

Aguirre de Carcer, at the time director of North American Affairs at the Spanish Foreign Ministry, provided a new formula. Carcer proposed to offer the United States continued base rights in exchange for a broad program of cooperation in nonmilitary fields, such as space tracking, peaceful nuclear development, education, culture, tourism, civil aviation, and investment, and, of course, the $175 million in aid. Carcer's formula deemphasized the close military ties for which Spain had previously asked. It allowed Spain to save face by getting more out of the agreement than mere rent payment, and provided an alternative for those in the United States who opposed close military ties with Spain.[39]

Carcer's new formula ended the stalemate. On June 21, 1969, the United States and Spain signed an interim agreement to extend American base rights until September 1970, while the two countries negotiated a series of separate agreements on educational, scientific, and cultural ties. Relieved to have the stalemate resolved, Spain lauded the extension agreement as a major diplomatic success. The Spanish press treated as a resounding triumph such small gains as agreement to keep in operation a committee to discuss mutual economic problems.[40] This emphasis on relatively insignificant points revealed how important the face-saving factor was to Spain.

The Detail Phase and the Outcome

With a new formula, and a new deadline, the two sides began working on specifics. But in early 1970, the contextual situation began to turn against the United States, weakening the American issue power position.

In September 1969, Colonel Muammar Qaddafi seized power in Libya and demanded that the United States evacuate Wheelus Air Force Base. The Soviet Union, which in recent years had substantially increased the size of its Mediterranean fleet, now seemed likely to gain at least port-of-call rights in North Africa. It is thus not surprising that in February 1970 the Pentagon completed a strategic review which concluded that the bases in Spain should definitely be retained.

By reducing American alternatives, and increasing American commitment, this new situation had increased Spain's issue power position. At the same time, Franco was acting to increase Spain's alternatives. In January 1970 Spanish Foreign Minister Gregorio Lopez Bravo, who had replaced the discredited Castiella, paid a brief visit to Moscow. Although his discussions there centered on potential commercial ties and did not lead to the reopening of diplomatic relations, the visit nevertheless represented a new flexibility in Spanish foreign policy. In February 1970, Spain completed an agreement to purchase thirty Mirage jets from France for $90 million.[41] By diversifying Spain's source of weaponry, this agreement also helped strengthen Spain's issue power position.

When the United States announced that it would move its Wheelus operations to the Spanish base at Zaragoza, Franco reacted by renewing his demand for some form of American security guarantee. Franco argued that the new Soviet threat in the Mediterranean increased the chances of Spain becoming a military target in an East-West conflict, and that Spain thus needed a formal security commitment.[42] When the Americans countered that the mood in Congress was not amenable to yet another foreign military commitment, Spain suggested a clever alternative. If the United States would not offer a firm security commitment, it should compensate by offering greater military aid and equipment.[43] Spain's enhanced issue power position had allowed it to reinsert the military component into the formula.

The Nixon administration considered an agreement strategically important, given perceived Soviet gains in the Mediterranean, but also knew that Congress would be wary of either a defense pact or more military aid. This uncomfortable situation led the United States to revive an option Franco had originally requested in 1952: Spanish membership in NATO.

On a visit to Madrid in June 1970, Secretary of Defense Melvin Laird unexpectedly endorsed the eventual entry of Spain into NATO. If agreeable to America's NATO partners, it would obviate the need to sign a bilateral defense pact with Madrid, while providing Spain with the security commitment it wanted.[44] But when he visited NATO capitals, Laird discovered that Franco was still not wanted. These feelings were particularly strong in Britain and the Nordic countries. Nixon was not eager to force Spanish membership, and within several weeks abandoned the effort.

With the deadline getting closer, the United States invented a compromise solution. The United States would offer as much of a defense guarantee as was possible without congressional approval, and would strengthen the Spanish military by providing it with a package of surplus American arms.

Spain accepted this alteration of the formula, and an agreement was quickly reached on August 6, more than a month before the deadline. The United States and Spain pledged that "each government will support the defense system of the other." This wording was less specific a security guarantee than a bilateral defense pact would have given, but a more specific one than provided in the 1963 extension agreement, in which each country had declared that an attack on the other would be "a matter of common concern."[45] The August agreement also set up a joint committee on defense matters and tied Spain's air defense system to NATO's. In addition, Spain was to receive $125 million over the next five years to buy military equipment, including thirty-six used Phantom jets, and an additional $60 million grant in the form of used American military equipment. Including some other miscellaneous items, such as sixteen used naval destroyers to be loaned to Spain, the total package was estimated to be worth between $300 million and $450 million.[46] It was less than Spain's original $1.2 billion request, but nearly three times as much as the initial U.S. offer in 1968.

Spain had succeeded in winning from the United States an agreement that went about as far as possible without congressional approval. In fact, the agreement caused considerable dissent within the United States. Senator J. William Fulbright, chairman of the Foreign Relations Committee, tried unsuccessfully to attach a rider to the military procurement bill to force Nixon to submit the agreement to the full Senate as a treaty. Fulbright argued that the wording of the defense guarantee was tantamount to a mutual defense treaty.

Although he could not have foreseen it at the time, Franco's decision to walk out of the talks in September 1968 had paid off. For between then and August 1970, contextual events caused the United States to reassess the value of Spanish bases. In hindsight, Carcer's proposal of 1969, which at the time appeared to be a face-saving Spanish concession, proved to be only a short-lived formula. Almost as soon as the two sides started negotiating the details of Carcer's formula, Spain began to see an opportunity unfolding to alter it; the negotiations thus quickly returned to a formula phase. The 1968–70 negotiations, then, saw four formulas put forward: bases for defense commitment (Spain's original objective), bases for rent (the incumbent formula, and the U. S. objective), bases for cultural ties (Carcer's formula), and finally, bases for a near-formal defense commitment and increased military aid and equipment.

Communicating Tactics

The principal Spanish tactic in this round of the negotiations was the threat of neutrality, which is another version of vetoing negotiations, the tactic Spain had used near the end of the 1951–53 talks. The difference is that whereas in the first round Spain, in frustration, had simply threatened to walk out of the negotiations, this time it couched the threat as part of a new foreign policy orientation. Also, it communicated it as a coolheaded foreign policy decision, unlike Franco's earlier emotional outburst.

But also unlike the earlier threat, it was communicated indirectly, albeit publicly, through a visiting West German, in tandem with a renewal of high-level contacts with Moscow. This gave the threat an air of uncertainty, as if the Spanish were not quite committed to carrying it out. In fact, as was soon revealed, there was considerable debate within the Spanish government as to whether a policy of neutrality was truly in Spain's best interests. When this schism became public, the threat lost credibility.

Its credibility was further undermined by the continuing greater issue power of the United States. Most important, U.S. commitment to an outcome favorable to Spain was low, and its alternatives were many. In short, even without the internal schism in Spain, there was no guarantee that the threat of neutrality would persuade the United States to change its position in the negotiations.

The United States had continued to follow a hard-line tactic of refusing to meet Spain's demands. When the first negotiation deadline came and went without significant American concessions, it was clear that the Spanish tactic had failed to persuade the United States, in contrast to the 1951–53 negotiations, during which Spain's threat to veto the talks succeeded in eliciting at least some concessions from the Americans. In the earlier instance, the tactic was communicated directly and credibly.

The outcome of this phase of the talks was the new face-saving formula, which can be seen only as a Spanish concession, since Franco was forgoing what he really wanted—economic aid and military ties—for what the United States was willing to offer—closer nonmilitary ties.

The sudden changes in contextual events over the ensuing months, however, proved immensely advantageous to Spain. For these changes not only decreased American alternatives and enhanced American commitment to Spanish bases, they also made Spain's tactic of threatening neutrality more persuasive. Before the weakening of American issue power, Spain's threats to walk out of the negotiations posed only minimal danger to the U.S. strategic position. With the changes, however, Spain's threat of neutrality caused greater alarm in Washington, and was thus more persuasive. This fact is apparent in the terms of the agreement of August 1970.

THE 1974–1976 NEGOTIATIONS

Negotiations for the renewal of the 1970 agreement began in November 1974. In the preceding several years, the American issue power position had weakened. The northern Mediterranean, from Portugal to Turkey, was viewed with concern in Washington. Euro-Communist parties were gaining strength in Italy and France, and Portugal barely averted a Communist-led coup in the spring of 1974. The Turkish invasion of Cyprus in August 1974 prompted Congress to withhold further military assistance to Ankara. The Turks responded by closing a number of American intelligence facilities. Greece, angered that the United States had not done more to forestall the Turkish invasion, withdrew Greek forces from NATO and ordered a reduction in the American presence in Greece. These contextual events reduced American alternatives, and increased American commitment to maintaining the bases in Spain.

Political developments within Spain also increased American concern. Even Franco's most ardent supporters knew he would not live forever, and when his health began to decline visibly in the early 1970s Spain became increasingly preoccupied with the politics of succession. In February 1974, members of the Basque separatist group ETA assassinated Prime Minister Luis Carrero Blanco. Because most observers regarded Carrero Blanco as the heir apparent to Franco, his assassination left a sudden vacuum in the Spanish hierarchy. In the summer of 1974, Franco designated the young Prince Juan Carlos as his successor, but little was known about the direction in which the prince would lead Spain. For the United States, "[t]hese events had the dual overall effect of creating uncertainty as to the political future of Spain at the very time that the value from a regional perspective of the U.S. military presence in Spain was enhanced."[47]

Spain's commitment, on the other hand, was waning. Since the early 1960s, the Spanish had become increasingly aware that, because of the American bases, their country would be a likely target in an East-West conflict. Further, the bases were also beginning to interfere with Spanish foreign policy objectives in the Arab world. During the 1973 Middle East war, Spain denied the United States permission to land and refuel planes airlifting supplies to Israel, and later made the United States pledge not to use the bases on missions in support of Israel. A poll conducted in the early 1970s revealed that only 16 percent of the Spaniards questioned wanted continued American use of the bases.[48]

When negotiations began Spain's objective was the by then familiar formula, bases in exchange for defense commitments and substantial aid. Specifically, Spain wanted a formal mutual defense treaty and between $1.5 and $2 billion in military aid and equipment. But this time, Spain was more optimistic that its demands would be met.

The Spanish opened with a new tactic. They warned that if their demands were not largely met, the United States might have to give up use of some of the bases.[49] For the first time since the 1951–53 negotiations the bases themselves became the subject of bargaining; until now, the negotiations had always centered on the amount and form of rent the United States would pay.

The negotiations proceeded slowly for the first ten months, at least in part because the United States was trying to gauge political developments in Spain. Washington was worried that a successor regime might repudiate an agreement with the Franco regime, clearly now on its last leg.

The United States thus made its usual argument that a formal defense treaty would not pass Congress. In response, the Spanish insisted that the United States must reduce its military personnel in Spain, and they placed their financial demand at "only" $1.5 billion. The United States then raised its aid offer from $500 million to $750 million.[50] At the

September 1975 deadline, the talks remained stalemated. Reverting to the tactic he had used in the negotiations for the 1953 agreement, Franco warned that he would not extend the September 26 deadline and that if no agreement were reached, U.S. forces must pull out by September 26, 1976.

Unfortunately for Franco, this tactic was rendered ineffective by what must have been one of his worst political miscalculations. On September 26, the negotiation deadline, Franco refused to commute the death sentences of five members of the Basque ETA group; the following day, the five were executed.

There was an immediate outcry from the rest of Europe. Every Western European country withdrew its ambassador from Madrid. Spain suddenly and painfully returned to the position of being Europe's outcast, the thing against which Franco had fought so hard since the end of World War II.

This event dramatically reduced Spain's issue power, for once again, as in 1950, the United States appeared to be its only potential friend. Henry Kissinger was quick to recognize this change, and on September 26 he warned the Spanish foreign minister that unless Spain moderated its negotiation demands, the United States would withdraw its political support.[51]

Kissinger's warning succeeded, and on October 4, 1975, the United States and Spain announced that they had reached "a new framework agreement governing cooperative relationships."[52] The agreement, to last five years, called for "some reduction" in the U.S. military presence in Spain and $500 to $700 million in U.S. military aid.[53] It left unclear the kind of mutual defense commitment, if any, that had been reached. This agreement represented a formula that exchanged continued use of Spanish bases for a moderate financial sum and a yet to be determined defense commitment. In other words, there was little difference between this formula and the one reached in 1970, except that the former promised to raise the rent payment by anywhere from $150 to $450 million, depending upon how the details were worked out.

But before negotiations over details could begin, the situation took another dramatic turn when Franco died on November 20. Reluctance to deal with Franco, the primary constraint on American commitment over the years, was suddenly removed. More important, confusion concerning the direction post-Franco Spain would take led to a sudden increase in U.S. commitment. The Communists' near coup in neighboring Portugal and evidence that the newly revived Communist party of Spain would play a major role in Spanish politics sent fears throughout the U.S. government that the bases might soon be removed no matter what the United States offered. The United States felt that greater American support for the young government of King Juan Carlos might help ensure that Spain would choose, and stay on, a democratic course. It was now in the Americans' interest to show that a democratic Spain could gain greater benefits from the United States than authoritarian Spain had been able to.[54]

The talks were thus speeded up, on American initiative, and by early 1976 a new agreement was signed. The United States agreed to provide Spain with over $1.2 billion in military credits and grants and, importantly, to make the new agreement a formal treaty of friendship and cooperation, subject to Senate approval. The defense commitment embodied in the agreement was now formal and unequivocal. By his death, Franco had finally achieved for Spain the outcome he had sought for over twenty years. In June, the Senate ratified the treaty, 84–11.

Conclusions: Power and Tactics

For twenty-five years, Spain had tried to create a formula that would trade bases for close military and political ties with the United States. Although the various agreements reached in 1953, 1963, 1970, and 1976 were each the result of a distinct negotiation, the series can be seen as one process. What changed from one negotiation to another was the context and, to a lesser degree, the issue power balance.

The 1951–53 negotiations were an example not only of a structurally weak actor negotiating with a structurally strong one, but of a structurally weak actor that also suffered a severe issue power weakness. When it opened negotiations with the United States, Spain had no alternatives and a strong commitment, but a commitment based on a desperate need for what only the United States could offer. The resulting issue power weakness proved impossible for Spain to alter significantly. Despite concerted attempts to alter the issue power balance—through concessions, pleadings, and warnings—Spain succeeded only in appearing even more desperate for an agreement. In the end, the threat to veto an outcome was Spain's most effective tactic.

America's issue power derived in part from its structural power—its many alternatives were based on its postwar global hegemony—and in part on domestic constraints on the American negotiators. The constraints provided U.S. negotiators with a convenient, though real, excuse for not giving Spain what it wanted. America's issue power advantage was evident in its primary tactic during the period. This tactic can best be termed an attitude of indifference. The United States forced Franco to make most of the moves, yet seemed unaffected by his tactics. Not until Spain threatened to end the negotiations was the United

States forced to play its hand, and admit to at least a modicum of interest in an agreement.

The resulting formula was far removed from what Spain had been trying to achieve. Instead of bases in exchange for close military and political ties, Spain had to settle for bases in exchange for an unspecified promise of future rewards. U.S. structural power was the basis of this promise, since it gave the United States the ability to offer many potential rewards. U.S. issue power was the reason Spain so quickly accepted such an unfavorable formula.

When the 1968–70 negotiations began, Spain again aimed for its ideal formula. This time, Spanish tactics centered on the threat of neutrality, which in effect was a form of veto, since it implied an end to the U.S.-Spanish relationship. But no substantial change had occurred in the issue power balance. American interest was low, perhaps even lower than it had been before, and equally constrained by the congressional and NATO factors. American alternatives remained high, and were buttressed by the development of nuclear submarine forces. The result was that Spain's tactic of threatening neutrality backfired. Once again, Spain had to accept a face-saving formula, this time one that redirected the terms of trade from bases for close military and political ties to bases for cultural ties.

This formula probably would have survived had it not been for the sudden contextual changes that occurred in 1969 and 1970. For the first time, America's issue power position was weakened, but not as the result of Spanish tactics. Rather, a perceived reduction in American alternatives gave Spanish bases a greater value to the United States, leading to a noticeable increase in American interest in Spanish bases.

This change in the issue power balance allowed Spain to alter the formula successfully, during what had begun as a detail phase, by reintroducing a substantial military component to the terms of trade. Although Spanish tactics had not caused the change in the issue power balance, Spain was quick to cash in on it. The final agreement thereby provided Spain with its greatest benefits to date.

By the beginning of the 1974–76 negotiations, the issue power balance had shifted even more in Spain's favor. It was now Spanish interest that was waning, and American interest that was growing. But again, the catalyst for the changed issue balance was contextual, specifically, American concern over its strategic position in the Mediterranean. Finally, with Franco's death, the remaining constraints on American negotiators were removed, opening the door to the formula Spain had always wanted: bases in exchange for a formal defense commitment.

The U.S.–Spanish bases negotiations were essentially negotiations over formulas. Once formulas were agreed to, working through their details proceeded relatively easily. This conclusion follows from an earlier observation: Spain was negotiating primarily for intangibles— recognition and acceptance by the West. Such intangibles are reflected in the structures of formulas, not in the minutiae of details. Thus, the right formula was the most important Spanish objective. As each series of negotiations began, Spain directed its tactics toward creating a new formula.

Yet Spain's tactics were, for the most part, ineffective in bringing about favorable formulas. The U.S. issue power advantage was so great that the only truly effective Spanish tactic was the threat to leave the negotiations. Not until certain contextual events started to increase American commitment and reduce American alternatives did the issue power balance change in Spain's favor. Even though Spain's leadership was quick to recognize and cash in on issue power changes, Spanish tactics were not their cause.

SIX

The Anglo-Icelandic Cod Wars

Between 1958 and 1976, Iceland successfully extended its fisheries limit from 4 to 200 miles. Each incremental increase—from 4 miles to 12, 12 miles to 50, and 50 miles to 200—was marked by fierce opposition from Britain, crisis confrontations, and negotiated agreements, virtually all of which endorsed Iceland's initial positions. In few other cases has a small state less ambiguously achieved its desired outcome in negotiations with a stronger state.

In 1952, Iceland had unilaterally extended its fishing limit to 4 miles upon the expiration of the 1901 Danish-British Fisheries Convention. The 1901 agreement, in which Denmark represented its Icelandic possession, had placed the fishing limit at 3 miles. From the time Iceland became an independent republic in 1944, the Icelanders began to express interest in expanding this limit.[1] When they did so in 1952, Britain angrily protested, and British trawler owners imposed a landing ban on Icelandic trawlers in British ports, although in 1951 Britain had accepted a similar fisheries extension by Norway.[2] The dispute was resolved in 1956, when the Consultative Assembly of the Council of Europe, to which the case had been referred in 1954, ruled in Iceland's favor. Britain lifted the landing ban on Icelandic trawlers and British trawlers started obeying the 4-mile limit.

Although this case is not considered here as one of the Cod Wars since there were no formal negotiations or crisis confrontations between the two states, it was nevertheless a harbinger of conflicts to come. Indeed, even before the 1952–56 dispute was resolved, Iceland already had begun planning for its next extension of the fisheries limit.

THE FIRST COD WAR, 1958–1961

On May 25, 1958, Iceland announced a unilateral extension of its fisheries limit to 12 miles, effective September 1. After that date, British and other foreign trawlers would be forbidden to fish within 12 miles of the Icelandic coast.

Iceland's objectives were simple and straightforward. It wanted to preserve as much of the surrounding fish stock as possible for its own fishermen. The fishing industry had accounted for between 15 and 20 percent of Iceland's GNP over the years, and was the cornerstone of the country's exchange economy. Between 1951 and 1955, fish and fish products accounted for nearly 95 percent of Iceland's total exports, and thus provided most of the foreign exchange Iceland needed to pay for imports of energy, machinery, vehicles, and virtually all other nonfish products.[3] Iceland possessed little else in the way of raw materials.

Given this dependence on offshore fisheries, Iceland wished to limit the catch size of foreign fleets. Between 1905 and 1955, Iceland's proportion of the total catch of fish off its shores had topped 50 percent only during World War II, when British and other European trawlers were inactive.[4] Recent decades had witnessed great advancements in fishing technology, which rendered foreign fishing fleets more efficient and increased their total catch per trip.

Moreover, Iceland had noticed alarming signs of overfishing in its waters. The total catch of demersal (bottom-feeding) fish had declined by nearly 16 percent between 1954 and 1957, despite an increase in the fishing effort.[5] Iceland sought to conserve what was seen as a diminishing fish stock, and felt its own fishermen should be allowed to reap the greatest benefit from what was left.

But Iceland's objectives were justified not solely by economic necessity. The Icelanders also felt that international law was progressing toward recognition of wider fishing limits. By 1958, seventeen states had expanded their coastal jurisdiction to 12 miles or more. The Conference on the Law of the Sea, meeting in Geneva in the spring of 1958, had determined that a state's territorial sea could not extend beyond 12 miles. The implication was that 12 miles was the upper limit, and that any extension up to 12 miles was legal.

Britain immediately challenged Iceland's unilateral extension of its fishing limit. The British government issued a declaration saying it would "not be able to accept the proposed decree . . . as of any effect in law," and warned that it would "prevent any unlawful attempt to interfere with British fishing vessels on the high seas."[6] Although Britain did offer to negotiate, its initial position was that the 12-mile limit was illegal and unacceptable; Britain's objective was to maintain the 4-mile limit.

Britain's objective also derived largely from economic sources. Though the fish industry accounted for less than one percent of the British GNP,[7] it was nevertheless of crucial importance to certain British communities, particularly the fishing ports of Humberside. It was estimated that 13 percent of the total British catch from all waters came from within the proposed 12-mile limit.[8] Though this figure does not reveal great dependence, it did translate into a substantial number of jobs on British trawlers and in British ports.

Like Iceland, Britain also argued its case on the grounds of principle. British boats had fished Icelandic waters since the 1300s.[9] Britain claimed that international law was on its side, and that Iceland could not unilaterally abrogate the 1956 ruling by the Council of Europe (though in fact the 1956 ruling did not have a specified duration).

Each side's initial position in May 1958 was clear. Iceland would accept nothing less than British acceptance of a 12-mile limit, whereas Britain would continue to respect only the 4-mile limit.

The Issue Power Balance

Iceland possessed few alternatives for achieving its desired outcome of preserving fish stocks and increasing its own catch. It could achieve the latter goal by expanding and modernizing its trawler fleet, or sending it to compete in distant fishing grounds, but this option would be costly for a nation of only 200,000 people. It could attempt to develop other industries to replace the fishing industry, but this option too would be difficult for a state with such little structural power. In short, the only real alternative Iceland had was to persuade the British to acknowledge and respect the 12-mile limit.

In one sense, this lack of alternatives was a source of issue power weakness, since it meant that Iceland's objectives could not be attained outside of its relationship with Britain. But in another sense, the lack of alternatives was a source of strength, since it bolstered the Icelanders' commitment. As was seen above, Iceland was almost totally dependent upon fishing for economic survival. Ever since independence in 1944, Icelanders of all political persuasions were unified in their desire to protect their fishing stocks and expand their fishing jurisdiction. Just as the Panama Canal was the one issue on which all political parties in Panama agreed, so was fishing the unifying issue in Iceland. The depth of Iceland's commitment was revealed by Prime Minister Hermann Jonasson, who in September 1958 explained Iceland's motivations: "We Icelanders could wait no longer. . . . fishing is more vital to us than any other nation, and we must, therefore, be entitled to the most favorable conditions in this field."[10] Or, in the words of a British observer who was sympathetic to Iceland: "If the fishing industry was important to Britain, it was vital to Iceland. Iceland's problem was not simply serious, but absolute."[11] If Iceland's problem was absolute, its commitment was equally so.

Another source of Iceland's commitment was alluded to earlier: principles and a sense of justice. As an increasing number of states expanded their territorial waters to 12 miles and beyond, Iceland, which was more dependent on fishing than any other state, felt justified in following suit.

Although justice is subjective—rare is the state that declares its own actions unjust—it is nevertheless true that people feel differing degrees of commitment to that which they feel is just. The Icelanders' belief that their actions were just was absolute, and contributed to their equally absolute commitment.

Iceland's control, the ability to achieve its outcome unilaterally, was limited, at least on paper. Iceland's Coast Guard was minuscule, and the 12-mile limit it hoped to enforce covered nearly 45,000 square miles of ocean. As will be seen below, Iceland developed a successful tactic of harassment which, though not allowing it to control outcomes, at least made Britain pay dearly for ignoring Iceland's demands.

Britain, endowed with considerably more structural power than Iceland, consequently had more alternatives. The British fleet was a long-distance one; it could and did trawl in fishing grounds throughout the North Atlantic. It was not inconceivable that Britain could replace the 13 percent of its catch that came from within 12 miles of Iceland's coast by increasing its fishing efforts elsewhere.

But pursuing alternatives usually involves greater costs; otherwise the actor would voluntarily choose the alternatives. The British had been fishing Icelandic waters for centuries. The fishermen knew the shoals around Iceland, and the domestic fish processing industry was geared toward handling an Icelandic catch. To be suddenly deprived of the Icelandic catch would thus involve significant, and costly, changes.

Still, Britain did at least have *potential* alternatives. But just as Iceland's lack of alternatives was a source of both weakness and strength, so Britain's possession of alternatives was a mixed blessing. Because Britain was only minimally dependent upon Icelandic fish, British commitment lacked the depth and fervor of Iceland's.

Nevertheless, certain groups in Britain did have a strong commitment to the government's position. The British Trawler Owners' Federation, as well as labor union locals in Humberside port cities, were fiercely committed to preserving their fishing rights in Icelandic waters. These groups lobbied the government to provide Royal Navy protection when Iceland began its tactic of harassment. But commitment in Britain, outside of these groups, was limited. As was noted above, the *entire* fishing industry accounted for less than one percent of

British GNP, and the catch from the disputed waters accounted for only 13 percent of that.

Britain's control over outcomes resembled its alternatives: substantial in theory, but limited in practice. The Royal Navy was somewhat less imposing than during the years of empire, but still much more than a match for the Icelandic Coast Guard. But like pursuing alternatives, exercising control entails costs. The British could easily have defended their fishing fleet in Icelandic waters, and indeed tried to do so to a limited extent, but not without substantially raising the marginal cost of Icelandic fish. Moreover, Iceland, as will be seen below, practiced tactics to ensure that British attempts at control would be as costly as possible. In the end, the British would have to decide whether defending its fishing rights off Iceland was worth the cost.

In sum, the issue power balance appeared at the outset to be in favor of Iceland, due to the Icelanders' great commitment and to the constraints on Britain's control. As the crisis wore on, Iceland's tactics would be directed toward raising the costs of British control and emphasizing the steadfastness of Icelandic commitment. Britain, on the other hand, would pursue tactics intended to undermine Icelandic commitment and exploit Britain's advantage in the control component of issue power.

Diagnostic Phase

The diagnostic phase essentially began after the 1956 agreement, since Iceland made it clear that the extension to 4 miles was only the first step in its expansion of its territorial waters. The British ambassador in Reykjavik, Sir Andrew Gilchrist, persuaded the Icelanders to postpone any further unilateral extensions until after the 1958 Law of the Sea Conference in Geneva.[12]

Nevertheless, the British began to consider the alternatives open to them if the Geneva conference failed to reach a consensus on territorial waters and Iceland proceeded with a unilateral move. Gilchrist reports that he and his superiors at the Foreign Office weighed the pros and cons of using the Royal Navy to defend British trawlers: "Unless the British warships were allowed to take 'effective naval action,'" Gilchrist writes, "it was difficult to see how we could win." But the constraints on using force were also recognized. For one, it was felt that world public opinion, or even British public opinion, would not countenance violent action. The British also realized that "[a]ny action which put at risk the NATO (really American) base in Iceland . . . must be excluded from consideration."[13]

This dilemma, which would confront Britain throughout all three

Cod Wars, was well expressed by Gilchrist: "*Firm* naval action was out of the question" but "*mild* naval action would do no more than postpone defeat."[14]

The Geneva conference failed to endorse a formal change, other than the tacit consensus to make 12 miles the maximum limit. In the final days of the conference, after it became clear that no consensus would be reached, the Icelandic foreign minister announced in a nationwide radio broadcast: "[Iceland] will take steps immediately after the end of the conference to extend further the 'fishing territorial waters.' . . . It has become obvious at the conference that a majority supports fishing limits that are considerably wider than hitherto."[15]

But even after the conference ended, Iceland did not take immediate action. Thus, for a brief time, the opportunity to negotiate remained. The British trawlermen, however, had been aroused by Iceland's announcement of an impending extension. They began calling for naval actions, landing bans, and other hard-line responses. In spite of Ambassador Gilchrist's advice to the contrary, the British government fell in line with the trawlermen, and refused to explore the possibility of bilateral negotiations.

London did, however, raise the issue at a NATO meeting in Copenhagen in early May 1958. The British hoped to apply diplomatic pressure on Iceland from within NATO. Though it was true that most NATO members were opposed to unilateral fisheries extensions, they were equally opposed to the British taking any action that might imperil NATO's unity. The Americans, in particular, were concerned that a British-Icelandic confrontation might lead to Iceland's closing of the NATO air base at Keflavik. Although the Icelandic government had not actually made such a threat, it was easy to imagine that a violent conflict with Britain could encourage them to do so.[16] Consequently, NATO refused to rally around the British, and in late May, Iceland formally announced its unilateral extension to 12 miles.

In effect, this was a "failed" diagnostic phase, as the two sides did not reach the decision to negotiate. But, as Zartman and Berman write, the search for a formula can begin even while the two sides are still diagnosing.[17]

The Search for a Formula

Initially, both Britain and Iceland put forward maximalist formulas, with zero-sum terms of trade. Iceland's formula was British recognition of the entire 12-mile limit, with nothing specified in exchange. Similarly, Britain's initial formula was for Iceland to continue abiding by the 4-mile limit, also with nothing specified in exchange. Clearly, one or both sides would have to move from its zero-sum conception of the formula if there was to be an agreement.

Britain moved first. In the summer of 1958, after Iceland had announced its intentions but before it had implemented them, the British government offered two alternative formulas. The first would replace the concept of territorial limits with one of yield limits. Specifically, Iceland would be guaranteed a certain total catch from the fisheries around its shore in exchange for allowing the British to fish unimpeded. The second alternative formula would grant Iceland a 6-mile limit, with mutually agreed upon conservation measures to be taken in certain areas outside of 6 miles.[18] Iceland rejected both of these alternatives, and continued to insist that the 12-mile limit was nonnegotiable.

Meanwhile, the British Trawler Owners' Federation announced that its members were determined to continue fishing within the 12-mile limit after September 1, and called on London to provide Royal Navy protection if Iceland resisted. Iceland responded by declaring that, as of September 1, Royal Navy penetration of the 12-mile limit would be regarded as an attack on Iceland.

Iceland's strong commitment was now clearly evidenced, both by its rejection of Britain's compromise formulas and by its stern response to the threat voiced by British fishermen. Iceland also pursued during the summer of 1958 a tactic to increase its alternatives. In August, Icelandic Minister of Fisheries Ludvik Josepsson traveled to Moscow to negotiate a $2.5 million loan from the Soviets, to be repaid in fish exports. The Icelanders, remembering Britain's landing ban during the 1952–54 disagreement, were indicating their commitment by preparing for a similar British response.[19]

On September 1, 1958, Iceland's new fisheries limit went into effect. British trawlers, as they had vowed to do, crossed the 12-mile line with a Royal Navy escort. The British trawlers concentrated in three groups, or "boxes," each of which was protected by Royal Navy frigates.[20] Icelandic Coast Guard vessels attempted to board British trawlers and arrest their crews; British frigates responded by trying to block, or even ram, the Icelandic boats. On September 26, Iceland announced that British vessels would no longer be allowed to dock at Icelandic ports, even in the event of medical emergencies.[21] The result was to increase Britain's costs of control.

Throughout the rest of 1958 and 1959, confrontations occurred on an almost weekly basis. During this period, Iceland refused to engage in formal talks, claiming it could not negotiate under duress. But both sides were looking to the second International Conference on the Law of the Sea, which was scheduled to convene in Geneva on March 17, 1960. It was hoped that the conference would reach a definitive decision on the legal limits of territorial waters. Iceland, of course, wanted the conference to declare that territorial limits of at least 12 miles were legal; Britain hoped for a lesser territorial limit. But even if the conference came out in support of Iceland's position, it would at least provide Britain with a face-saving way to end the Cod War.

The conference, however, failed to reach a decision. Britain immediately began to take steps to enhance prospects for a negotiated solution. On April 28, 1960, the British announced that Royal Navy vessels would withdraw temporarily from inside the 12-mile limit. They hastily added, however, that this action was taken only to encourage a peaceful resolution to the conflict, and did not mean British acceptance of the 12-mile limit.[22]

Why was Britain suddenly willing to make this concession in order to enhance negotiations? In part because of the failure of the Law of the Sea Conference. It was clear that if and until a new conference convened, the two sides would have to reach a settlement on their own. But another factor was the growing costs to Britain of pursuing the Cod War.

After only the first ten months of the Cod War, a total of 5,000 British navy men and 37 ships of the fleet had patrolled Icelandic waters.[23] Although it was never revealed how much this effort cost the British Treasury, it is doubtful that it was very much less than the value of the fish caught in the disputed 8-mile band. Moreover, fishing in the protective "boxes" was cumbersome, and hardly the most economically efficient way to trawl. And in spite of these protective measures the Icelandic Coast Guard vessels, manned by expert seamen, had still been able to disrupt British fishing significantly. As Ambassador Gilchrist wrote, "It was not a way of defeating the Icelanders. And, of course, it was a very expensive way of not defeating them."[24]

When Iceland still refused to negotiate, Britain made another concession in May 1960. The British Trawler Owners' Federation, with prodding from the government, agreed to a three-month fishing truce, during which time they would withdraw beyond the 12-mile limit. But again, the British insisted that this truce was not to be seen as acceptance of Iceland's position.

On August 10, 1960, two days before the truce was to expire, Iceland agreed to hold formal talks. This was a concession of sorts, since agreement to hold talks implied that Iceland's maximalist formula was perhaps more flexible than it appeared. But by agreeing to hold talks, Iceland gained a pledge from the British to extend the fishing truce for as long as negotiations were underway. Iceland could thus enjoy de facto British recognition of the 12-mile limit while the search for a formula continued.

Talks were held throughout the fall and early winter of 1960–61. By this point, it had become apparent to the British that Iceland would not back down on the 12-mile limit. The issue for Britain became whether to accept Iceland's formula, which offered a zero-sum terms of trade, or create a formula that would provide Britain with at least something in exchange for accepting the 12-mile limit. Actually, the British had no choice. They had to create a new, face-saving formula. To accept Iceland's initial formula now, after over two years of costly confrontation, would be seen as an unambiguous defeat. The British trawler owners might very well have chosen to ignore such an agreement, thus putting the government in an extremely uncomfortable position.

Yet the issue power balance was still in Iceland's favor. The Icelanders had demonstrated their commitment and their ability to render costly Britain's attempts at control. Moreover, if no agreement was reached soon, the fisheries truce would end, and the situation would return to one of confrontation. And there was no evidence that renewed confrontation would cause Iceland to back down; in fact, the evidence provided by the past two years was to the contrary.

So on December 21, 1960, British Foreign Secretary Lord Alec Douglas-Home proposed a new formula in a letter to his Icelandic counterpart. Britain would agree to the 12-mile limit, but only in an agreement that provided "assurance that any dispute on future extensions of fishery jurisdiction beyond 12 miles would be referred to the International Court of Justice."[25] Britain was offering a formula that would offer British recognition of Iceland's 12-mile limit in exchange for an Icelandic promise not to make a similar unilateral move in the future.

The Icelanders were slow to respond to Lord Home's proposed new formula. Their immediate response was that it was under consideration. After over a month went by without an Icelandic response, Lord Home sent another message via the British ambassador in Reykjavik. In it, Lord Home said that he was "seriously disturbed by the probable consequences of failure to achieve a settlement in the very near future," and warned that unless a settlement was reached within two weeks, "a critical and dangerous situation would arise."[26] The "dangerous situation" of course referred to the return of British naval vessels to Icelandic waters, with an inference that this time they would be more aggressive in protecting British trawlers. The tone of this second letter suggested that Britain felt it could not accept anything less than the new formula. London had to come away from the Cod War with something, if only an Icelandic promise not to provoke a future Cod War.

As favorable as the new formula was to Iceland, it was, nevertheless, the topic of intense debate within the Icelandic government. There were those who believed that, since Iceland's fisheries extension was totally within the bounds of international law, there should be no agreement at all with Britain.[27] In the end, however, after barely surviving a no-confidence vote in the Icelandic Parliament, the Icelandic government accepted the British formula.

The British threat had evidently served its purpose. The Cod War confrontations were costly for Britain; they were also costly for Iceland. The Icelandic Coast Guard comprised only six small ships, some of which were damaged after being rammed by the Royal Navy. The Icelanders could, and did, make fishing difficult for British trawlers; but they could not totally prevent the trawlers from fishing, assuming Britain was willing to incur the costs involved. Lord Home's threat implied that Britain was willing to continue incurring these costs if no agreement were reached.

The Outcome

Once the formula was accepted, an agreement quickly followed. There were few details to work out, since the only real issue in the negotiations was one of principle: Did Iceland have the right to extend unilaterally its fishing limit to 12 miles? Because principles fall under the domain of formulas, the formula itself could be implemented as a final agreement.

On February 27, 1961, the agreement was formally announced. It contained the following points:

1. The United Kingdom would no longer object to a 12-mile fishing limit around Iceland.

2. For a transitional period of three years British trawlers would be allowed to fish in the greater part of the zone between 6 and 12 miles off the Icelandic coast at specified seasons of the year, the seasons varying from one part of the coast to another.

3. The base lines from which the fishing limits were measured would be modified in Iceland's favor.

4. Iceland would undertake to give six months' notice of any proposal to extend its new fishery limit, and any dispute arising from such a proposal would be referred to the International Court of Justice at the request of either party.

The outcome was a victory for Iceland, since it more resembled Iceland's initial position than it did Britain's. Even Iceland's major concession, the agreement to refer future extension proposals to the International Court, was not so significant as it might have seemed. For many people believed that within several years international law would come to recognize territorial water limits of even greater than 12 miles as being the norm. If so, then Iceland's future obligation could prove to be but a formality.

Iceland fared so well because of its greater commitment which allowed it to accept the costs of the confrontations with British trawlers. When, after eighteen months of such confrontations, the Icelanders had still not altered their initial demands—and in fact had not even agreed to formal negotiations—it was only a matter of time before Britain was forced to offer concessions.

For Britain, the question all along had been how great a price should be paid to preserve fishing rights in an 8-mile band of ocean. Faced with Iceland's tactic of harassment, Britain in the end was willing to accept a face-saving formula, but even that had to be accompanied by a threat, so great was Iceland's commitment.

THE SECOND COD WAR, 1971–1973

In June 1971, Iceland, after the formation of a new left-wing government, declared that effective September 1, 1972, the country's fisheries limit would be extended to 50 miles. In doing so, the government formally abrogated the 1961 agreement with Britain.

Iceland's objectives and motivations were essentially the same as in 1958: a desire to increase Icelanders' share of the catch in the face of foreign competition and perceived overfishing. The argument was best expressed by Foreign Minister Einar Agustsson:

> The proposed extension was essential, reasonable, natural, fair and just. Essential, because the fish stocks in Icelandic waters were threatened with imminent ruin from overfishing by the world's distant water fleet. Reasonable, because every state should have the right to utilize its own natural resources. Natural, because the continental shelf, the platform under the sea, on which the 50 mile limit was staged, was an integral part of the country's territory and the fish stocks were a natural resource in precisely the same way as oil beneath the sea-bed. Fair, because Iceland has no other natural resource to speak of. Just, because only the states most concerned would effectively protect and conserve the fish stocks for the benefit of all in the absence of any agreed international law for fisheries.[28]

Iceland also argued that the extension was warranted because of changed circumstances, specifically, the development of electronic devices to locate fish. Such devices enabled trawlers to fish more economically and more productively, thus depleting the fish stocks at a greater rate.

As for the 1961 agreement, Iceland claimed that it had been made under duress, thus rendering it void under the Vienna Convention on the Law of Treaties.[29] This was a curious argument, however, since the

1961 agreement had been in force for ten years with Iceland's apparent consent.

Iceland also argued on principle, as it had in 1958, by pointing out that since 1960, twenty-five states had extended their fishing limits beyond 12 miles, and some by up to 200 miles. In other words, since there was no generally accepted limit under international law, Iceland had as much right as any other state to decide its ocean boundaries.

Britain protested Iceland's unilateral move by arguing that the 1961 agreement was still valid, and that Iceland should thus refer its decision to the International Court. Moreover, the British felt that Iceland, and any other state considering an extension in its territorial waters, should wait until the United Nations Conference on Maritime Law, scheduled for 1973.

In addition to these arguments based on principle, Britain also admitted to economic reasons for opposing Iceland's move. In a parliamentary debate on July 20, 1971, the British undersecretary of state for Foreign and Commonwealth Affairs, Anthony Royle, claimed that "the proposed 50 mile limit would include virtually all the fishing grounds in the Icelandic areas, and the exclusion of our vessels from them would deprive us of between one-fifth and one-quarter of all British landings of such species as cod, haddock and plaice." Royle said the move would deprive Britain's distant water fleet of between 40 percent and 60 percent of its catch, and that it was unlikely very much of this could be made up for elsewhere.[30]

The British thus faced a greater potential economic loss if Iceland's newest extension came into force than they had with the earlier 12-mile extension. The extension from 12 to 50 miles would add another 90,666 square miles of ocean from which British trawlers would be excluded (they were excluded from 45,000 square miles under the 1961 agreement).[31]

Once again, the two sides were putting forth maximalist formulas. Iceland was demanding outright British acceptance of the 50-mile limit; Britain was insisting the old formula should remain in force, at least until Iceland abided by its terms and presented its case to the International Court.

The Issue Power Balance

Iceland's commitment to preserving its fishing industry and its fish stocks remained as deep in the early 1970s as it had been in the late 1950s. Fishing was still the backbone of the Icelandic economy, accounting for 86 percent of the value of exports during the period 1966 to 1970. Furthermore, although the 1961 agreement had tripled Iceland's share of the catch, it had risen by only 25 percent in the ensuing ten years.[32] The Icelanders thus felt that in relative terms they were losing ground to foreign fleets. Indicative of the extent of Iceland's commitment is the unanimous vote of the Althing, or Parliament, in favor of the 50-mile extension. Clearly, the fisheries issue remained the unifying force in Icelandic politics.

The alternatives available to Iceland in 1971 were few, just as they had been in 1958. It was inconceivable that a state with the minimal structural power of Iceland could have easily replaced an industry of such paramount importance as fishing. But could Iceland have achieved its objectives—preserving the fishing stock and protecting the domestic industry—by some means other than unilateral extension? The 1961 agreement called for Iceland to submit any requests for a fisheries extension to the International Court. But Iceland had no faith in either the Court or the upcoming Maritime Law Conference. The record of such transnational meetings was poor; questions of fisheries jurisdiction had often been on their agendas during the past decades, and yet no generally recognized limits had been established. In short, the Icelanders felt the only option with a chance of success was another unilateral extension.

One factor that accounted for this belief was the seemingly high control component, based on the outcome of the first Cod War. Iceland had demonstrated then that it possessed the ability to harass British trawlers to the point of rendering their efforts too costly to bear. Admittedly, Iceland faced a taller order in 1971—the defense of a 50-mile, instead of a 12-mile, band of ocean. And in the interim, the Icelanders had not substantially increased the size of their coast guard. Nevertheless, harassment does not require a large force, particularly when the activity is taking place in home waters. Moreover, Iceland had in recent years developed a "secret weapon"—the trawl cutter—which, as will be seen below, partially made up for the asymmetry in force size. Finally, the first Cod War demonstrated that, in the words of one observer, "the Cod Wars were never a test of military strength but, due to the strategy and tactics applied, first and foremost a delicate test of excellence in seamanship."[33] On this score, the Icelanders always enjoyed an advantage.

Britain's alternatives for achieving its desired outcomes were, like Iceland's, few. The extension of Iceland's fisheries limit to 50 miles would deprive Britain of a sizable portion of its distant waters catch, too sizable to be easily replaced by fishing elsewhere. Britain could, and did, protest to the International Court and the Maritime Law Convention, but without Iceland's consent these bodies were powerless. Britain thus had no options for achieving its outcomes other than negotiation, or confrontation, with Iceland.

The British in 1971 were somewhat more committed than they had been in 1958. The reason is obvious. Their potential loss was much greater. Whereas in 1958 the British stood to lose 13 percent of their fishing catch from Iceland's 12-mile extension, they would lose between 40 and 60 percent from the 50-mile extension, and between 20 and 25 percent of their total catch of cod, haddock, and plaice, the staples of Britain's fish and chips shops. Thus, the 1958 extension was injurious to only a segment of the fishing industry (the segment based in the Humberside ports), but the new extension would have a much broader impact, not only among those in the fishing industry, but among the British population at large through a noticeable increase in fish prices.

Another factor contributing to Britain's commitment in 1971 was the widespread, and valid, belief that Britain had lost the first Cod War. The 1961 agreement was seen for what it was: a face-saving way for Britain to withdraw from a hopeless situation. Now the Icelanders were trying to dupe the British again, only this time to a much greater extent. As will be seen below, more aggressive tactics on the part of the Royal Navy in defense of British trawlers was evidence of Britain's commitment.

Yet Britain's commitment was less strong than Iceland's. For Iceland's commitment was based on an absolute need to protect its predominant industry. But fishing accounted for an even smaller proportion of British GNP in 1971 than it had in 1958. Another factor serving to constrain Britain's commitment was the support of certain groups in Britain for Iceland's move. Britain's inland fishing industry, for example, favored expanded fisheries limits, since, like Iceland, it wanted to limit foreign fishing in home waters. As a result, Britain would find it more difficult to present a unified front in negotiations.

The first Cod War revealed how little unilateral control Britain had in achieving its objectives. Although Britain's navy was still substantially larger than Iceland's coast guard, there were serious constraints on its being used as a fighting force. Foremost among these was reluctance to exchange fire with a NATO ally, a constraint that Iceland was to use to its advantage during this second Cod War. Also, as in the first Cod War, Britain faced high costs in exercising control, and Iceland, armed with its new trawl-cutting device, had now raised those costs even more.

Thus, in 1971, Iceland maintained its issue power advantage. Its unmatched commitment and its ability to inflict unbearable costs on British trawlers would once again prove to be the decisive factors. Iceland's tactics would again be directed toward emphasizing commitment and inflicting the greatest costs possible on both British control and British commitment. In addition, Iceland for the first time would attempt to escalate the scope of the issue by threatening the stability of the NATO alliance.

The Search for a Formula

Britain and Iceland began holding talks on the dispute in November 1971, ten months before the new limit was to go into effect. In January 1972, the British put forward the first of several compromise formula proposals. They proposed that Iceland retain the 12-mile limit in exchange for Britain promising to limit its catch within the 50-mile limit to the average annual catch of the period 1960 to 1969 (210,000 tons).[34] The Icelanders rejected this formula, since it was the size of the foreign catch between 1960 and 1969 that had provoked them to extend the limit in the first place. They offered instead an alternative equally unacceptable to Britain: Iceland would allow British trawlers to continue fishing within the 50-mile limit for a specified period of time after September 1972, but under the condition that Britain agree to recognize the limit and eventually to phase out all fishing within it. Lady Tweedsmuir, minister of state for Foreign and Commonwealth Affairs and one of Britain's negotiators, claimed that "to negotiate an arrangement on this basis would have been to concede Iceland's right to control the waters out to fifty miles and to jeopardise our future fishing."[35] In essence, each side's alternative was simply a restating of its initial, maximalist position, albeit with minor modifications.

The negotiations thus returned to stalemate. The British, however, began voicing warnings and threats. Anthony Royle, in a House of Commons question period on March 6, 1972, said: "I cannot say that we would in no circumstances resort to naval protection for our fishing vessels."[36] Less equivocal was the warning of Austen Laing, director general of the British Trawler Owners' Federation, who warned that British trawlers were prepared for a second and "fiercer" Cod War if Iceland proceeded with its extension.[37]

Talks resumed in the late spring and early summer. With a new Cod War looming, the British offered a second version of their alternative formula, in which they would limit their catch to 185,000 tons a year in exchange for Iceland retaining the 12-mile limit. Iceland rejected this version as well, and put forth a new offer of its own. A limited number of British trawlers, of a specified size, would be allowed to fish in certain designated areas of Icelandic waters in exchange for British recognition of the 50-mile limit. Iceland estimated that its proposal would allow

British trawlers to catch approximately 138,000 tons. Britain summarily rejected this suggestion.[38]

The problem with this exchange of formulas was that neither side was conceding on the major issue, the fisheries limit extension. Britain was trying to create a formula that made concessions on catch size but kept the fisheries limit at 12 miles; Iceland was willing to allow minimal British access to Icelandic waters, but only in return for recognition of a 50-mile limit.

On July 14, 1972, the talks broke down. Iceland returned to its original positions, and prepared to enforce the 50-mile limit. British trawlermen prepared for the assault, and received assurances from London that, in the event of serious harassment, the Royal Navy would intervene. On September 2, 1972, between 60 and 70 British trawlers crossed the 50-mile limit. On September 5, the Icelanders first successfully employed their secret weapon—the trawl wire cutter—to the dismay of the British fishermen. Trawl wire cutting was an extremely effective means of harassment. Fishing boats, because of their size, can carry only one trawl. If the trawl wires are cut, the boat not only loses the fish already caught in the net, but must also return to its home port for a new trawl. By its use of the cutter, Iceland had greatly increased the cost of British efforts at control.

Talks resumed in Reykjavik in early October, but to no avail. The British government, under pressure from the trawler owners, launched a series of threats. Anthony Royle warned Iceland that the use of the British naval force was "close at hand," and called on the Icelandic government "to match our restraint and sanity."[39] But the Icelanders saw how effective the tactic was, and the harassment continued throughout the fall.

On October 21, British dockworkers declared a ban on all imports from Iceland arriving on Icelandic ships. This action, however, only increased Icelandic commitment. The Icelandic government said it would immediately seek new markets for its fish, and would assist any other Icelandic industries affected by the ban. Iceland's prime minister vowed that the ban would not have "the slightest effect on our trade situation."[40] Iceland's commitment remained strong.

Meanwhile, British commitment was being weakened by Iceland's harassment. British trawler owners were crying for more aggressive naval protection. The British government was faced with either making concessions in the negotiations or escalating the Cod War to a new, more violent level. They took the former course. On November 26, a British delegation was sent to Reykjavik with a new offer, which implied British acceptance of Iceland's 50-mile limit. It called for one-third of the waters within 50 miles of Iceland's shores to be closed at any given time, and the British catch to be limited to 163,000 tons.[41] This formula contained both limited access and limited catch, but more important, it tacitly recognized Iceland's newly proclaimed fisheries extension, since its calculations were based on a 50-mile limit. Britain had made a major concession. The search for a formula now focused on what rights Britain would retain in Icelandic waters, not on the legal extent of those waters.

On November 27, Iceland responded by proposing that one-half of its waters be closed to British trawlers, and that, moreover, only British trawlers of less than 180 feet in length or under 800 tons in weight be allowed access to the other half. The British rejected this counteroffer, pointing out that it would reduce their catch to only 62,000–83,000 tons, but offered to add to their proposal a 10 percent reduction in the number of fishing days by British vessels, which would reduce the British catch to an estimated 158,000 tons. Iceland stood firm, and the talks broke off again.[42]

In the first several weeks of 1973, Iceland intensified its harassment tactics. The limited harassment in the fall of 1972 had led to a major British concession, as discussed above. Iceland now returned to that tactic in an effort to elicit even more concessions from London. By the middle of January, British trawler owners were finding the harassment almost unbearable. They demanded Royal Navy protection, and vowed to move out of Icelandic waters if protection was not forthcoming. The British government agreed to send a civilian support ship within Icelandic waters to protect the trawlers, but shied away from deploying naval vessels. The British were clearly reluctant to deploy the Royal Navy against a NATO ally. Sir Alec Douglas-Home, the British foreign secretary, told Parliament on January 22: "There are British naval vessels capable of doing the job, but once we begin to use the Navy for protection . . . that is the beginning of a 'cod war.' "[43] Because of British reluctance to send in the navy, Iceland maintained its issue power advantage.

Iceland's harassment tactics crossed a critical threshold in March and April 1973 when, for the first time, Icelandic gunboats opened fire on British trawlers. Although the shots were intended to frighten, and not harm, the British government responded with two tactics, one hard-line and one soft-. The hard-line tactic was encompassed in a new series of threats. In response to a question in Parliament, Sir Alec Douglas-Home said: "I am sure that the policy of restraint has been right up to now. There is a limit to patience. The Icelandic Government had better know it."[44]

The soft-line tactic was an offer to renew ministerial level negotiations. Iceland consented, and talks were held in Reykjavik on May 3 and

4. Britain, which had tacitly accepted Iceland's 50-mile limit, now wanted to discuss a formula whereby Britain's rights within that limit would be based on total catch size. Specifically, the British offered to limit their catch within the range of 117,000 to 156,000 tons (their earlier offer had limited their catch to 163,000 tons).

But Iceland was still searching for a formula that would limit British access. They offered to divide Icelandic waters into six pockets, with three being open to British trawlers at any given time. This proposal was essentially identical to their offer of November 1972. In any event, Iceland wanted to keep the British catch below 117,000 tons. Neither side was willing to move, and the talks ended in failure.[45]

In the face of the continuing stalemate, Britain on May 19 ordered the Royal Navy to provide protection for British fishermen inside the 50-mile limit. The Icelandic government called the decision "a hostile act taken against an ally which is defending its vital interests by protecting its main natural resources."[46] Iceland recalled its ambassador to London and said that negotiations would not resume so long as the Royal Navy was in Icelandic waters.

Numerically, the Royal Navy had a clear advantage over the Icelandic Coast Guard. A total of 14 Royal Navy ships with 1,854 officers and men were deployed in Icelandic waters, compared with 7 Icelandic Coast Guard vessels with only 139 officers and men.[47] But the Royal Navy had orders not to fire live ammunition. Their mission was limited to preventing trawl wire cutting by blocking or ramming the Icelandic ships. The Icelanders were still able periodically to cut trawl wires. Since the damage caused by cutting trawl wires was so great, Iceland did not require a high success rate to make its harassment tactic effective.

Nevertheless, Iceland was not pleased with the new escalation of the Cod War. Although Iceland's commitment was still strong, its own costs of exercising control were increased by the deployment of the Royal Navy. A number of Icelandic Coast Guard vessels were severely damaged by British ramming. But instead of this leading to Icelandic concessions, Iceland chose to raise the stakes by adopting a new hard-line tactic.

This tactic was playing Iceland's NATO card. On May 21, two days after the Royal Navy entered Icelandic waters, the Reykjavik government registered a formal protest with the NATO Council in Brussels. Simultaneously, Iceland announced that British military aircraft would no longer be allowed landing rights in Iceland, even if on NATO missions. Several days later, the Icelandic government went so far as to threaten to leave NATO and close NATO's American-manned air base at Keflavik. An Icelandic government spokesman asserted that his government would regard NATO's response to Iceland's protest as "a test case. . . . It will show whether NATO is there only for militarily strong nations, or if there is something in it for Iceland too."[48]

Iceland's threats to leave NATO, or at least to hinder its operation, were highly credible, in part because of Iceland's very high level of commitment, but also because of the composition of the coalition government formed in 1971. This leftward-leaning government included several cabinet members from parties ideologically opposed to Iceland's membership in NATO. Ludvik Josepsson, the fisheries minister, was a member of Iceland's Communist party. Some observers thus felt that Iceland might even have been using the dispute with Britain as a convenient excuse for withdrawing from NATO.[49]

Iceland was employing a tactic weak states often use effectively: expanding the scope of the issues. In taking their complaint to the NATO Council and, more important, in hindering NATO operations by denying the British Air Force landing rights, Iceland was hoping to reduce British commitment by bringing NATO pressure to bear on London. This tactic can be seen as a form of coalition building, since Iceland was, in effect, trying to force the other NATO members to become its allies on the issue.

These moves, combined with growing worldwide press attention the Cod War was receiving (most of it favorable to Iceland), were causing immense discomfort in London. Indicative was the British government's publication and dissemination, on June 21, 1973, of a White Paper outlining the British position.[50]

Clashes between Icelandic Coast Guard boats and Royal Navy frigates continued throughout the summer, while on the negotiation front the stalemate continued. Although the pressure was mounting, neither side wanted to back down. In fact, Iceland, its commitment unwaning, prepared to raise the stakes even further. In September, the Icelandic government began hinting that it might close the NATO air base at Keflavik. These hints were sufficiently strong to provoke a visit to Reykjavik by NATO Secretary General Dr. Josef Luns. To top off their hard-line tactics, the Icelanders announced on September 26 that unless the Royal Navy and British trawlers departed Icelandic waters by October 3, diplomatic relations would be severed.

With no sign that Iceland was about to back down, and upon the urgings of Dr. Luns, who held talks with Prime Minister Edward Heath immediately after his trip to Iceland, Britain offered a concession on October 2. In a message to Icelandic Prime Minister Olafur Johannesson, Heath offered to withdraw British naval ships from Icelandic waters under the condition that Iceland allow British trawlers to continue fishing. Such was Iceland's issue power strength at this point that

Prime Minister Johannesson turned down the offer, saying he could not discontinue enforcing Icelandic law in Icelandic territory. And such was Britain's issue power weakness that Prime Minister Heath, on October 3, decided to withdraw the Royal Navy anyway.

This final concession by Britain, which in effect acknowledged Iceland's victory on the field of play (the fishing grounds), also signaled to the Icelanders that they would most likely get their way in the negotiations as well. For it was unlikely that Britain would make such a major concession in the Cod War if it was not prepared also to make concessions in the negotiations.

Indeed, when the two prime ministers met in London on October 15 and 16, the British accepted the Icelandic formula—exchanging British recognition of the 50-mile limit in return for limited British access to Icelandic waters.[51]

The Detail Phase and the Outcome

As in the first Cod War, the acceptance of a mutually agreed upon formula was tantamount to reaching a complete agreement. The detail phase consisted of determining what specific parts of Icelandic waters would be open to British fishing. The parties agreed to do so in such a way as to provide Britain with a total catch of 130,000 tons, almost the exact midpoint of the 117,000 to 156,000 ton range the British had offered in the spring.

The formal agreement reached in November included the following main points:

1. The waters between 12 and 50 miles off the Icelandic coast would be divided into six rotating areas, five of which would be open to British trawlers at any given time, and each of which would be closed to British vessels for two months each year.

2. In addition, three conservation areas would be closed at certain times each year, and three other conservation areas would be permanently closed to British trawlers.

3. A maximum of 68 British trawlers of more than 180 feet in length, and 71 of under 180 feet, would be allowed to fish Icelandic waters. The total of 139 ships was 25 percent fewer than had fished in Icelandic waters in 1971.

4. The agreement would last for two years, in the expectation that in the interim the Law of the Sea Conference would be able to establish firm fisheries limits.[52]

Although it was not a point of the agreement, the British also agreed to lift their landing ban on Icelandic products.

Iceland had once again secured an advantageous agreement. It had gained British recognition of the 50-mile limit and had reduced the British catch from 208,000 tons in 1971 to 130,000 tons. Once again, Iceland's commitment was the principal source of its issue power advantage. This commitment allowed Iceland to respond to Britain's deployment of the Royal Navy not by conceding but by raising the stakes even higher.

In the face of this intense commitment on the part of the Icelanders, Britain had little choice but to concede. Because the Royal Navy was given orders not to fire on Icelandic boats, Britain's structural advantage in the control component of issue power was severely handicapped. The constraints on Britain actualizing its full power of control, that is, by actually firing on Icelandic ships, derived largely from its NATO relationship with Iceland, a relationship that Iceland used to its advantage.

In sum, Iceland maintained an issue power advantage throughout the second Cod War. The Icelanders rarely conceded on either the field of play or in the negotiations. The British, however, did not recognize the fundamental implications of their defeat. When a new Cod War broke out in 1975, the British returned to the tactics they had used unsuccessfully in the two earlier confrontations.

THE THIRD COD WAR, 1975–1976

The third Cod War began in much the same way as the earlier two, with a unilateral Icelandic extension of its fisheries limit, this time to 200 miles. The new limit, which was announced in the summer of 1975, was to go into effect on October 15. Britain, however, would continue to enjoy the terms of the 1973 agreement until it expired on November 14.

Iceland's motivations were by now familiar. The government argued that overfishing had reached a dangerous point, particularly overfishing of cod, which comprised over 80 percent of the British catch in Icelandic waters in recent years. In 1954, the total cod catch was 547,000 tons; by 1974 it had fallen to 374,000 tons, despite more efficient fishing methods. Icelandic scientists estimated that, unless conservation efforts were made, the total cod catch could drop below 100,000 tons by 1990.[53]

On top of the familiar problem of overfishing, Iceland was suffering through an economic crisis. Inflation in 1975 rose to over 50 percent, primarily because of rising energy costs. Moreover, during 1974 there had been a dramatic fall in world fish prices, thus reducing Iceland's export earnings, of which fish still accounted for 75 percent. As a result, Iceland's trade deficit in 1974 had climbed to 12 percent of its GNP.[54] In short, in the words of Iceland's minister of fisheries: "If the Icelanders are to keep up with other nations with living standards, their share in the total fisheries on the Icelandic fishing banks must increase."[55]

Iceland's arguments on the basis of principles had also grown in recent years. Many countries had already claimed 200-mile economic zones, with exclusive or preferential fishing rights. Brazil had done so in 1971, Argentina in 1973, and Mexico and Norway were in the process of implementing 200-mile limits. The United States Senate also had approved a 200-mile extension, and was awaiting the House of Representatives' vote. During the 1973 meetings of the Sea Bed Committee of the United Nations, a total of thirty-four states called for international recognition of coastal states' rights to 200-mile exclusive zones.[56] Iceland thus had strong reasons to believe that its unilateral extension was within the bounds of international law.

Britain's opposition to the extension centered more on economic reasons than on questions of legality. The British fishing industry was in a state of crisis. Between January 1974 and June 1975, over one hundred British trawlers had gone bankrupt.[57] If Iceland was successful in extending its fishing limit to 200 miles, there would surely be many more bankruptcies in the British fishing industry.

The British argument on the grounds of principle and justice, which had been strong in 1971 and stronger still in 1958, was significantly weaker by 1975. As discussed above, the international community was steadily progressing toward recognition of 200-mile limits. In fact, the British were considering a significant extension in their own fishing limit. In May 1975, the British Trawler Owners' Federation called for a 100-mile exclusive fishing zone, with another 200 miles open only to EEC (European Economic Community) member countries.[58]

Because of the general acceptance of the legality of the 200-mile limit, negotiations in the third Cod War focused almost entirely on what rights Britain would retain within that limit. In this sense, the third Cod War negotiations were based on the same formula that had been created in the second Cod War: British recognition of Iceland's fisheries limit in exchange for limited British access. By extending its fishing limit to 200 miles, Iceland had altered the parameters of the old formula, but not its terms of trade. The 1975–76 negotiations, then, focused almost entirely on details. But unlike the detail phases of the earlier negotiations, which were short and relatively tranquil, the third Cod War negotiations witnessed the most heated confrontations yet.

The Issue Power Balance

Iceland maintained its issue power advantage in the third Cod War. British commitment was higher than it had been in the preceding confrontations for the economic reasons already mentioned, but it was still not absolute, as was Iceland's. High commitment translates into a capability to withstand greater costs and to raise the stakes of a conflict without damaging national unity. As will be seen below, Iceland's tactics reflected this capability.

The control component of issue power also favored Iceland. Although extending their fishing limit to 200 miles gave the Icelanders even more water in which they needed to exercise control, they had learned in the second Cod War that they could inflict severe costs on the British even with their limited capability. The British should have learned from the earlier Cod Wars the limitations of their own ability to exercise control, at least with sustainable costs. Instead, they resorted to the same tactics and thus suffered the same consequences.

Negotiations over Details and the Outcome

Negotiations began in London in June 1975 in an attempt to reach a settlement before the new extension went into effect. Iceland initially offered to allow limited British fishing within the 200-mile limit, but to end all British fishing within the 50-mile limit. Britain wanted to retain rights within the 50-mile limit by renewing the 1973 accord, and then negotiate fishing rights within the 200-mile limit. The British did not, however, openly question the legality of the 200-mile zone. With their opening positions on the table, and neither side willing to move, the negotiations broke off.[59]

Negotiations resumed in Reykjavik on November 15, two days after the new limit went into effect. The British, as they had done in the earlier negotiations, turned the focus of the talks from access to catch size. Specifically, they offered to reduce their catch from 130,000 tons (as under the 1973 accord) to 110,000 tons, with details of access to be worked out later. Iceland responded by saying that the maximum British catch it would allow was 65,000 tons, and that this catch must come from outside the 50-mile range. The talks broke off again.

Meanwhile, events on the field of play were following the by then familiar course: British trawlers continued to fish in Icelandic waters and called for Royal Navy support. The Icelanders condemned Britain's "hostile acts" and said negotiations could not resume while British ships were in Iceland.

The Icelanders also began pursuing a course they had followed at the end of the second Cod War. On November 26, the Icelandic government closed its air space to Royal Air Force aircraft. Iceland had thereby chosen to play its NATO card much sooner than it had before.

Early December saw a number of serious confrontations between

British frigates and Icelandic Coast Guard boats. The British were clearly concerned with the course the conflict was taking. On December 11, British Foreign Secretary James Callaghan met with his Icelandic counterpart, Einar Agustsson, at a NATO meeting in Brussels. Callaghan offered to renew negotiations "at any place, at any level, at any time." Furthermore, he told Agustsson that Britain was willing to accept a catch figure below 100,000 tons. Agustsson, however, insisted that the 65,000-ton limit was "final and not negotiable." More important, Agustsson warned that the continued presence of British warships in Icelandic waters "could easily result in such extensive damage to the NATO cause in my country that no Icelandic Government would be in a position to counter it effectively." This warning was directed not only at the British, but at the other members of NATO as well. The Icelanders had clearly noted the great success with which they had ended the second Cod War by employing the NATO linkage.[60]

Iceland carried this tactic one step further on January 12, 1976, by announcing that it would leave NATO and break diplomatic relations with Britain if British ships did not leave its waters.

This rapid escalation in the war of threats took Britain by surprise. On January 19, Britain agreed to redeploy its warships (but not its trawlers) outside the 200-mile zone and invited Icelandic Prime Minister Geir Hallgrimsson to London for talks with Prime Minister Harold Wilson. During these talks, Britain conceded even more, offering to limit its catch to 85,000 tons. Hallgrimsson, however, remained adamant, arguing that Iceland's fish stocks were so low that "there were no fish left for the British."[61]

When the Royal Navy returned to Icelandic waters in early February, after a series of successful Icelandic trawler wire cuttings, Iceland followed through on its earlier threat and severed diplomatic relations, the first time such an action had happened between two NATO members. It also reiterated its threats to withdraw from NATO. The Icelandic press carried editorials arguing that NATO membership was of no benefit to Iceland if it could not even prevent aggression by another NATO ally. The anti-NATO sentiment began to gather significant public support in the early months of 1976. A number of protests and demonstrations took place outside the American NATO base at Keflavik. The leader of the main opposition party in the Icelandic Parliament jumped on the bandwagon, declaring in a parliamentary speech: "I find it extremely difficult to tolerate that we Icelanders sit in cooperation with Britain in [NATO] at the same time as they are inflicting such aggression on us in Icelandic waters."[62]

This public sentiment in Iceland buttressed the government's credibility that it would carry out its threat. It also sent chills through NATO. Josef Luns, secretary general of NATO, stated during the crisis that it would cost $22 billion to establish an observation system equal to that provided by Iceland's Keflavik base.[63] Indeed, Keflavik was of crucial importance in monitoring Soviet naval movements in the North Atlantic and was NATO's chief lookout over the Greenland-Faroes gap, the route Soviet ships would use to enter the Atlantic from their base at Murmansk.[64]

The third Cod War was thus becoming a major embarrassment for Britain, since it was now threatening to lead to a significant strategic reversal for NATO. Yet the British were in a bind. The talks had broken off indefinitely, and their trawlers were pleading for greater protection. As a result, the Cod War heated up during the spring of 1976, with several serious collisions taking place in April and May. Moreover, the costs of Britain's attempts at exercising control in Icelandic waters were mounting. The British had deployed a total of twenty-two frigates to protect their trawlers. It was estimated that a fleet of this size cost about £40 million a year to maintain. Yet the total value of the 1975 British catch in Icelandic waters was only £23 million.[65] Thus, not only was the Cod War threatening the unity of NATO, it was also proving to be extremely costly to the British treasury.

By late May, it became even more evident that Iceland was committed to carrying out its threat to leave NATO. Several Icelandic officials went on record as saying that an agreement was "out of the question" because of the latest increase in confrontations, and Foreign Minister Agustsson said on May 20 that it was now "extremely likely" that Iceland would withdraw from NATO.[66]

The following day, British Minister of State Anthony Crosland met with Agustsson in Oslo. Iceland now had the upper hand; Britain simply wanted the dispute to end. On May 30, the two sides announced that talks would reopen in Oslo on the 31st. Within twenty-four hours, a new agreement was reached. So desperate were the British to wash their hands of the whole affair that they accepted terms that would limit their total catch to only 30,000 tons, 35,000 below Iceland's initial offer in the fall of 1975. Furthermore, the agreement would be in force for only six months, after which British trawlers would have access to Icelandic waters only with the approval of the Icelandic government.[67]

The accord signed on June 1 limited the number of British trawlers allowed to fish in Icelandic waters to no more than twenty-four per day, delineated certain conservation areas in which British trawlers would be banned, and granted Iceland the right to stop and question any British trawlers it felt were violating the agreement. Like the second Cod War agreement, this agreement was structured in terms of access, even though the negotiations had focused on catch size. There was a practical reason. It would be difficult for Iceland to monitor catch size if British trawlers were granted unlimited access. It was much easier to negotiate a catch size limit, and then structure access limitations accordingly.

COMMUNICATING TACTICS

The First Cod War

Both Iceland and Britain practiced tactics of coercion during the first Cod War confrontation. Coercive tactics are the actualization of threats. Yet, unlike threats, there is no ambiguity as to their credibility; coercive tactics are credible if they are carried out. But all coercive tactics are not equally persuasive, since credibility does not guarantee persuasiveness. Similarly, not all coercive tactics cause the opponent to change his behavior. Thus, though both sides' tactics were credible, Iceland's proved to be more persuasive and effective.

Each side entered the confrontation espousing a hard-line position and threatening to employ coercive action. Britain, however, had offered concessions in an effort to fend off a confrontation. Although the British renewed their hard-line rhetoric when Iceland rebuffed these concessions, the offer of concessions nevertheless indicated that Britain was not completely committed to its professed position. It would later weaken the persuasiveness of British tactics.

Britain's coercive tactic consisted of violating Iceland's newly proclaimed 12-mile fishing limit. As noted above, it was a credible tactic because it was carried out. But it was not persuasive; it did not change Iceland's position or affect Iceland's coercive tactic of harassing British trawlers. It was not persuasive for two reasons. First, Iceland was willing to incur the costs of British coercion. Iceland's response with its own coercive tactic indicated that the Reykjavik government was even prepared to raise the stakes. Second, Britain was not willing to escalate its coercion, even though it possessed the requisite structural power capability. This unwillingness derived in part from the costs such escalation would involve, costs that would be out of proportion to the possible benefits, and in part from a reluctance to worsen hostilities with an erstwhile NATO ally.

It soon became evident that Britain's coercive tactic was ineffective, and was in fact only boosting Iceland's commitment. Iceland's coercive tactic, on the other hand, succeeded in changing Britain's perception of the crisis. Specifically, the British began to realize that they were locked into a stalemate Iceland was willing to prolong indefinitely. This realization led to some unilateral British concessions, such as the three-month fishing truce, in hopes of eliciting corresponding concessions from Reykjavik. But these concessions only encouraged the Icelanders to maintain their hard-line position. In the end Iceland, prodded by Britain's last-minute warning, made sufficient concessions to allow the British to escape with a face-saving formula.

The Second Cod War

The tactical pattern of the second Cod War was similar to that of the first: Both sides used coercion to support hard-line opening positions; Britain once again offered unilateral concessions in the face of an unacceptable stalemate; Iceland, interpreting British concessions as a sign of weakness, continued its coercive tactic until it achieved its objectives. The only changes from the first conflict were Britain's escalation of its coercive tactic by firing on Icelandic Coast Guard ships, and Iceland's concomitant initiation of its NATO tactic.

Britain's decision to deter more aggressively Iceland's tactic of harassment, combined with more strident British threats, raised the level of coercion. This move threatened to make the stalemate more costly to Iceland. The objective, of course, was to encourage Iceland to make concessions, something that Britain's earlier unilateral concessions (such as acknowledging Icelandic jurisdiction in the 50-mile zone) had failed to do. But Iceland responded to this intensified British coercion by adopting a new tactic—threatening to withdraw from NATO.

Britain's attempt to raise the level of coercion had backfired, for it prompted a new Icelandic tactic which brought pressure to bear on London from states other than Iceland. Once again, Britain was persuaded to accept that the stalemate could end only on Iceland's terms. The rapidity with which Britain conceded following Luns's visit to London was evidence of the effectiveness of Iceland's tactics in changing British behavior.

The Third Cod War

The tactical exchange of the third Cod War continued the pattern of the second, only the sequence of events moved more rapidly. Mindful of how the NATO tactic had successfully ended the second Cod War, Iceland played this card much earlier this time. Moreover, the tactic's credibility was enhanced by even greater anti-NATO sentiment among the Icelandic people and by a more visible effort by Luns to persuade Britain to end the conflict. As in the earlier confrontations, British concessions were unmatched by Iceland, and British coercion failed to alter Iceland's position, so that the only remaining option was to concede defeat.

CONCLUSIONS: POWER AND TACTICS

The three Cod Wars are a vivid example of how a state weaker in structural power may nevertheless enjoy an issue power advantage. They also show that no matter how much the structural power asymmetry favors one of the actors, the issue power asymmetry may be equally great in favoring the other actor. Moreover, as hypothesized in chapter 2, the issue power balance plays a greater role in determining the outcome of negotiations.

Iceland's issue power advantage was based on its great commitment to achieving its desired outcome. It is difficult to stress too strongly the depth of the Icelanders' commitment to protecting their ocean resources. Icelandic leaders constantly described the fishing disputes as threats to Iceland's very survival. Though certain segments of the British population were also strongly committed, the commitment of the British nation as a whole came nowhere near to matching the absolute commitment exhibited by Iceland.

Another source of Iceland's issue power advantage was Iceland's ability to neutralize effectively British attempts at control, primarily because the field of play was in Iceland's home waters. Iceland's attempts at control thus came at a considerably lower cost than did Britain's. This advantage allowed Iceland to practice the tactic of harassment, a tactic that structurally weaker states can usefully employ to weaken the stronger state's commitment and control.

In addition to harassment, Iceland also used two other tactics effectively: a hard-line negotiating posture and a tactic of linkage building. The hard-line negotiating posture was possible because of Iceland's strong commitment, which ensured domestic consensus. Iceland's uncompromising position forced the British to attempt to exercise control, thus provoking crises in which Iceland had the ultimate advantage. Because they knew that in the long run Britain could not maintain the costs of protecting its trawlers, the Icelanders did not feel a strong need to compromise in the negotiations.

But the most effective Icelandic tactic was that of broadening the scope of the issue by creating a linkage between its conflict with Britain and its relationship with NATO. Iceland first used this tactic in the second Cod War, and it was instrumental in ending the conflict.

As for Britain, although it had an immense structural power advantage, it was never able to develop tactics to translate this power so as to alter the issue power balance. The British tactic of sending the Royal Navy to Icelandic waters was not only costly relative to the stakes involved, but also severely constrained by British reluctance actually to use force. One of the reasons Iceland's tactic of linkage was so successful is that it served to constrain the British even further. Iceland's brinkmanship, breaking diplomatic relations and threatening to leave NATO, put the British in the position of having either to escalate the crisis further or make concessions. The Icelanders provided the British with no middle ground. In parliamentary debate following resolution of the third Cod War, Anthony Crosland succinctly described Britain's dilemma:

> What were the alternatives? There was in fact only one. That was to continue to pursue the cod war, with the certainty of dangerous escalation, with international and especially NATO opinion moving sharply against us, at a mounting cost in terms of naval protection, with our moral position steadily eroding as nation after nation accepted the principle of 200 miles.[68]

One of the questions the Cod Wars raise is why the British never seemed to grasp Iceland's favorable issue power balance. The British pursued essentially the same tactics in all three incidents despite the evidence after the first and second incidents that these tactics were not effective. This reveals the difficulty structurally stronger states have in recognizing that the issue power balance may not be in their favor. Even after the third Cod War, many in Britain decried the government's "abject surrender" to Iceland.[69] But the 1976 agreement did not represent British surrender. Rather, it represented British defeat at the hands of an actor whose power position in the particular issue in question was substantially greater than Britain's.

The three Cod Wars demonstrate the importance of principles as a source of commitment, and thus of issue power. In the first Cod War the Icelanders were slightly ahead of the rest of the world in announcing extended territorial waters. But by the second and third Cod Wars Iceland's position was compatible with what had become the mainstream view. Commitment is thus not always based solely on desire and the need for a certain outcome. It may be based equally strongly on a sense of justice and principle.

SEVEN

Conclusions: Findings and Implications

The objective of this study has been to analyze asymmetrical international negotiation, defined as negotiation between states with greatly divergent structural power resources. The emphasis has been on understanding how power is manifest under conditions of asymmetry, and on how both weak and strong states employ negotiation tactics to attain their desired outcomes. The assumption throughout has been that negotiation outcomes are a function of the actors' power.

In chapter 2, we presented a framework for analyzing power in negotiation as a three-dimensional concept: Aggregate structural power is an actor's total resources and capabilities; issue power describes an actor's resources and capabilities within the context of a specific issue or relationship; and tactical (or behavioral) power is an actor's ability to use its power resources to attain objectives. Our initial hypothesis was that, in interstate negotiation, the nature of the actors' issue power balance largely determines the process and outcome. Further, the objective of tactical power in negotiation is to alter the issue power balance in a more favorable direction.

Using this analytical framework of power, and the formula/detail processual framework, we took a close look at three case studies. The cases were similar in that they all featured aggregate structural power asymmetry. Yet there were also some important differences, most notably in the nature of the issue power balance. The Panama Canal negotiations showed great fluctuations in the balance (though the general trend was in Panama's favor). Throughout the Spanish bases negotiations, the balance more often favored the strong actor (the United States). And in the three Cod Wars, Iceland (the weak actor) constantly enjoyed a favorable issue power balance. There were also differences in the choice of tactics. Finally, there were differences in the outcomes—the weak state negotiating with complete success in one case (the Cod Wars), with much success in another (the Canal negotiations), and with only moderate success in the third (Spanish bases).

In this final chapter we will move from the specifics of the individual cases to the general principles they reveal. Specifically, what do they tell us that may be relevant for analyzing other cases? What guidelines do they imply for negotiation practitioners? What are the implications of our findings for international relations theory?

Findings

Issue-specific structural power is the most critical component of power in asymmetrical negotiation.

The case studies confirmed our hypothesis that the negotiation process consists of efforts by both sides to change the issue power balance. Moreover, there was a direct connection between the nature of the issue power balance and the outcome of the negotiation. When the issue power balance was consistently in favor of the weak actor (the Cod Wars), the weak actor achieved virtually all of its objectives. When the issue power balance fluctuated (the Canal negotiations), there was no clear "winner." And when the issue power balance unambiguously favored the strong actor (the Spanish bases negotiations), the strong actor achieved more of its objectives. Virtually every tactic employed was directed toward affecting one or more of the components of issue power—alternatives, commitment, and control.

These three components of issue power are the most important elements in the negotiation process. Thus, any attempt to predict a negotiation's outcome, monitor the status of an ongoing negotiation, or assess the outcome of a completed negotiation must focus on an analysis of the actors' respective alternatives, commitment, and degree of control, and the tactics they adopt to affect these elements.

Control is the single most important component of issue power.

Control was defined in chapter 2 as the degree to which an actor can achieve its objectives unilaterally (i.e., outside the negotiation context). The two cases in which control was a factor (the Canal negotiations and the Cod Wars) showed a direct relation between an actor's degree of control and its success in achieving its desired outcome. Iceland enjoyed a great advantage in control (and skillfully used tactics to enhance this advantage), and thus enjoyed a more favorable issue power balance and a more successful outcome. In the Canal negotiations, Panama fared best when control seemed to be shifting in its favor (for example, after the 1964 riots). But the U.S. military presence in the Canal Zone guaranteed a minimum degree of American control which Britain could never achieve even with its warships in Iceland's waters. The fluctuating issue power balance in the Canal negotiations reflected the great uncertainty surrounding the control component.

In both cases the "field of play" was on the weak actor's turf. This fact greatly enhanced Panama's and Iceland's efforts at bolstering their control. Thus, a corollary finding is that *the greater a weak actor's proximity to the "field of play," the more enhanced are its attempts at increasing its control.*[1]

The resources of aggregate structural power may increase alternatives and control but cannot increase commitment.

Aggregate structural power resources can increase an actor's alternatives, and thus its issue power. In the early years of the Panama Canal negotiations, the United States used the threat of employing its aggregate structural power resources to build a new canal as a means of "correcting" the issue power balance, which had shifted in Panama's favor in the wake of the 1964 riots. Similarly, the U.S. capability of constructing bases anywhere in the world, and providing the host country with substantial financial remuneration, provided the United States with a constant source of alternatives to bases in Spain. As these two examples show, alternatives can often be bought. The actor with greater aggregate structural power has an important advantage, since its financial resources can be used to give credibility to its alternative-building tactics.

There are times, however, when alternatives cannot be bought. Britain, for example, could not use its aggregate structural power to develop alternatives to Icelandic fish because the abundance of Iceland's fishing grounds was unique and could not be found elsewhere at a viable cost. Even a state with the aggregate structural power of the United States sometimes reaches limits on its ability to buy alternatives. When it became clear in the early 1970s how much a new Central American canal would actually cost, the U.S. ability to create alternatives to the Panama Canal quickly diminished. Nevertheless, in general, the strong actor will have a greater ability to increase its alternatives.

The resources of aggregate structural power can also enable the strong actor to increase its control. The ability to achieve outcomes unilaterally can derive from military force and coercion or from otherwise ignoring or resisting the opponent's demands. But even if aggregate structural resources exist, the actor may face severe constraints on using them to increase control. These constraints may derive from internal public or political opposition to coercively increasing control, or the costs of increasing control may be greater than the likely benefits. These constraining factors were evident in both the Panama Canal and

Cod War cases, in which neither the United States nor Britain used its full potential to increase control. If the constraints are sufficiently great, then aggregate structural power resources become less effective in affecting the control component of issue power.

The one area in which aggregate structural power resources have clearly no effect is in increasing commitment. Commitment cannot be "bought," nor can it be increased through coercion. Commitment is based partly on aspiration and need, and partly on the tactical ability to motivate one's constituency. In fact, greater aggregate structural power may actually hinder attempts to increase commitment, since a strong actor may have less need of an outcome and thus more difficulty rallying its constituency.

The implication, borne out by our case studies, is that commitment in the sense of aspiration is the weak actor's best hope for creating and maintaining a favorable issue power balance. It is the one component of issue power that cannot be increased by aggregate structural power resources.

Because a weak actor generally has more at stake in negotiation with a strong actor, it will devote more attention and energy to achieving its desired outcome.

Joseph Nye writes of the "asymmetry of attention" and the resulting "greater cohesion and concentration" of the weak actor.[2] These factors were evident in all three of our case studies. For Panama, Spain, and Iceland, the negotiations were the most important issue on their foreign policy agendas and the preoccupation of their foreign policy bureaucracies. Each state's regime enjoyed widespread public support for its position, true even for Panama and Spain, where the regimes were not otherwise universally popular.

The "asymmetry of attention" greatly enhances the weak actor's issue power position. For one, it helps increase and sustain commitment, particularly in the face of a hard-line position by the strong actor. Moreover, it enhances the credibility of the weak actor's tactics. It was easier for Torrijos to threaten the United States with violence when he knew that the Panamanian elite, bureaucracy, and populace shared his view and would rally to his support in the event he was forced to carry out the threat. Iceland's leaders knew that their tactic of harassment, though costly, would receive support from all sectors of Icelandic society.

It is unlikely that the strong actor can devote as much attention, or develop as much cohesion, as the weak actor. The strong actor has many issues on its foreign policy agenda, all of which have particular constituencies within its foreign policy bureaucracy. A conflict with a weak actor is probably not a strong state's foremost concern (the U.S.– North Vietnam conflict is a notable exception). In each of our case studies, moreover, opinion within the strong state about its position in the negotiations was divided. Some in the United States strongly sympathized with Panama's desire for sovereignty over the Canal, and others felt the Canal was an integral part of the United States and should never be the subject of negotiation. Some groups felt that U.S. bases in Spain were critical to Western security, and others felt that avoiding contact with the Franco regime could best enhance Western security. The British government also had a hard time developing an internal consensus in its conflict with Iceland, partly because the issue affected few people in Britain and partly because many British empathized with the Icelanders.

The "asymmetry of attention" thus helps a weak actor overcome the asymmetry in aggregate structural power. It maintains and strengthens, and at the same time derives from, the actor's commitment. There are two drawbacks, however. First, if the asymmetry is too great, the weak state will constantly be trying to get the strong state's attention. For though greater attention works to the weak state's advantage, the strong state must pay at least *some* attention to the problem or negotiations will never get off the ground. Second, the strong state, because it is likely to be involved in more relationships and have more interests, may fear that any concessions it makes to the weak state will have an adverse precedent effect in its other relationships. Many Americans, for example, felt that concessions to Panama would be interpreted as weakness by other countries in which the United States had interests.

The weak state can bring about a change in the issue power balance only through the use of tactics not based on aggregate structural power.

Since a weak actor does not possess the aggregate structural power resources to alter greatly the issue power balance, it must rely on tactics whose effectiveness and credibility derive from other sources. Examples of such tactics from our case studies include coalition building, based on the ability to find allies and persuade them to join your case; harassment and threats of disruption, based on territorial advantages and commitment; and threats to veto the negotiations, based on the nature of the negotiation process. None of these tactics requires the tangible resources of aggregate structural power.

The weak state fares better in negotiations in which it is defending against a perceived injustice by the strong state.

Both Panama and Iceland felt that the opponent was violating their sovereign rights. On balance, they negotiated more effectively than the Spanish, who were trying to get the opponent to enter, not leave, Spanish territory. A negotiation position based on defense of territory or rights has two advantages for the weak state. First, it strengthens and broadens commitment, which, as we have seen, is the weak state's best hope for altering the issue power balance in its favor. It is easy to rally people around a perceived injustice or threat.

Second, it makes it easier for the weak state to threaten sanctions against the strong, thus broadening its range of tactics. Panama was able to pose a threat to Americans in the Canal Zone as well as to the continued operation of the Canal itself. Iceland also could pose a threat to its stronger opponent, since British trawlers in Icelandic waters provided a convenient target. In the Spanish bases negotiations, on the other hand, the threat of sanctions was not a tactical option for Spain; the Spanish were trying to lure the Americans in, not drive them out.

Obviously, whether the weak state feels itself defending against the strong or not depends upon the issue; it is not a condition that can be created. But if the condition exists, the weak state often can accrue the resulting tactical advantages.

Real or perceived weakening of the strong state's aggregate structural power can alter the issue power balance in the weak state's favor.

If during the course of a negotiation a real or perceived weakening occurs in the strong state's aggregate structural power, the weak state may benefit at the issue power level. In effect, the bilateral relationship becomes less asymmetrical. An example of a real weakening in aggregate structural power is the case of Britain throughout the three Cod Wars. During this period, Britain's weakening position was quantitatively evident: GNP per capita, industrial production, Britain's share in world trade and defense spending all fell, and the British pound lost its status as the world's preeminent currency. Furthermore, Britain's decline as a great power was much commented upon and widely recognized, especially by the British themselves.

An example of a perceived decline in aggregate structural power is the case of the United States during the Panama Canal negotiations. Although in quantifiable terms the United States remained the world's greatest power, events such as the Vietnam War and the OPEC price increases helped produce the impression of declining American preeminence, an impression compounded by a critically self-reflective mood within the United States.

A real decline in the strong state's aggregate structural power affects the issue power balance in two ways. First, it reduces the strong state's ability to employ the resources of aggregate structural power to bring about favorable changes at the issue power level. Specifically, it limits the strong state's ability to increase its alternatives or control. Britain's rapid decline throughout the Cod War years rendered British efforts at control more and more costly. Britain's relatively quick acceptance of Iceland's complete demands in the final Cod War indicates that by then the British themselves had come to realize how limited was their ability to control events in Icelandic waters.

Second, a real decline in the strong state's power boosts the weak state's morale and commitment, both of which are usually greater than the strong state's to begin with. Iceland's confidence and assertiveness noticeably increased from one Cod War to the next.

Both effects allow the weak actor to practice a wider range of tactics and to be more daring in its tactical behavior. To put it simply, the weak state can get away with more.

A *perceived* decline in the strong state's aggregate structural power can also affect the issue power balance. If the weak state believes that the strong state's position has weakened, it may behave *as if* the strong state now has less ability to increase its alternatives and control. That is, it may adopt more hard-line tactics. Sometimes these tactics succeed: Panama's more aggressive tactics in the immediate post-Vietnam years eventually produced a favorable formula. But these tactics, since they are based on a perceived and not a real decline in the strong state's power, may backfire: Argentina's fateful decision to occupy the Falkland Islands in 1982 provoked an unexpectedly harsh response by a Britain that was not so weak as the Argentines thought. But even a perceived decline in the strong state's aggregate structural power increases the weak state's morale and commitment. And that increase alone leads to a more favorable issue power balance.

Contextual events and systemic changes may critically affect the issue power balance.

Contextual events and systemic changes can have a profound effect on the issue power balance. Though this is not a particularly profound analytical finding, it is often not taken into account and is thus worth discussing.

The U.S.–Spanish bases negotiations offer several examples. These negotiations resulted from the converging interests of the United States and Spain in light of the systemic changes caused by the growing Communist challenge. Before the 1968–70 negotiations, the issue power balance altered in favor of the United States as a result of another systemic development, the introduction of ballistic missile–firing nuclear submarines. And before the 1974–76 negotiations, contextual events in the Mediterranean led to an issue power balance more favorable to Spain. The actors foresaw none of these events. Yet in each instance, the United States and Spain adopted tactics and negotiating positions that took advantage of the favorable contextual changes.

These examples from the U.S.–Spanish bases negotiations are of tangible systemic changes (Communist gains, new strategic missiles, and instability in the Mediterranean). But intangible systemic changes, such as changes in international values and norms, can also affect the issue power balance. For example, during the course of the Panama Canal negotiations, strong state intervention in the affairs of the weak grew less acceptable by the international community. Realpoliticians might argue that this change should not have limited American tactical options. But the facts speak otherwise. Despite a long history of intervention in Central America in previous decades, between 1964 and 1977 the United States never even threatened to coerce Panama with military force. Similarly, during the course of the three Cod Wars, international acceptance of expanded territorial waters undermined Britain's position.

An extended discussion of the factors determining international values and norms is not in order here. Nevertheless, values and norms are constantly changing. A simple change of regime or government in a major state may lead to a new set of norms. For example, had Ronald Reagan been president of the United States during the Canal negotiations, American intervention in Panama might have been more likely. Margaret Thatcher's actions in the Falklands conflict suggest that she might have felt less restrained in responding to Iceland's harassment tactics had she been prime minister during the Cod Wars.

Negotiations conclude when one or both of the parties feel that the costs of an agreement are less than the costs of further altering the issue power balance.

The question of closure is critical to understanding the negotiation process. Why do negotiations end when they end? What causes the two sides to cease tactical exchanges and accept an agreement?

Negotiation agreements always involve costs. Each side must concede on some issues and accept less than it may have wanted originally; there may be domestic political costs to the government or regime; and there are costs of implementing the new agreement and establishing a new relationship. But the negotiation process—each side's attempts to alter the issue power balance—also involves costs. Increasing alternatives and control uses resources; increasing and sustaining commitment depletes political energy; and a drawn-out negotiation process will begin to interfere with a government's ability to focus on other important foreign and domestic issues. When one or both parties feel that the costs of negotiating have become greater than the costs of reaching an agreement, closure will occur.

If only one party makes this assessment, it will accept the opponent's most recent offer. Britain, for example, realized near the end of the third Cod War that continuing its efforts to alter the issue power balance would pose unbearable costs, including the military costs of trying to increase control and the political costs deriving from Iceland's tactic of coalition building within NATO. Iceland, however, gave all indications that it was both capable of and willing to continue paying the costs of not having an agreement. As a result, the British had no choice but to accept Iceland's last (and not very generous) offer.

In the 1951–53 U.S.–Spanish bases negotiations, the Franco regime made a similar calculation. To Spain, the costs of not reaching an agreement would have been carrying out its threat to end the talks, thus ending all hopes of establishing a new relationship with the United States. The United States was apparently willing to accept a rupture in the negotiation process if the alternative was accepting Spain's demands for close ties. Closure was reached when the Spanish concluded that accepting the American offer (limited as it was) was preferable to paying the costs of not reaching an agreement.

The Panama Canal negotiations were different in that both sides determined that an agreement would be less costly than continuing the negotiation process. For the United States, this realization began to come after the Security Council meeting in Panama City. For Panama, it came during the hiatus caused by the U.S. presidential election campaign, when economic pressures on the Torrijos regime began to build and the United States appeared to be hardening its position.

But each side knew that the other was in a similar position, and neither wanted to accept the opponent's most recent offer out of hand. The problem thus became one of timing: When does one close if both sides want an agreement and an end to the costs of tactical exchanges, but neither wants to close first?

The answer is that one closes slowly, with each side attempting to squeeze a little more out of the other before the inevitable agreement. Sometimes this works; the United States was able to get Panama to accept a permanent American role in Canal defense. And sometimes it fails; Panama was not able to get the United States to agree to its last-

changing, for such changes may mark a critical turning point in the negotiations.

How do each side's tactics affect the issue power balance?

The analyst must determine how particular tactics affect the issue power balance, that is, how they affect alternatives, commitment, and control. He or she will also want to determine why particular tactics are more useful for affecting certain components of issue power and how the opposing side responds to these tactics' effects.

How is the issue power balance altered after tactical exchanges?

Detecting changes in the issue power balance is the key to understanding the negotiation process, since that process consists of a series of changes in the issue power balance until a final balance (or outcome) is achieved. Therefore, after each tactical exchange, the analyst should reassess the issue power balance and ask: In whose favor has it altered? Are the actors aware of the change? Has the change made an agreement more or less likely?

What effect do changes in the issue power balance have on the negotiation process?

After determining how the issue power balance has changed, the analyst must address the impact this change has on the negotiation process. For example, how does it affect ensuing concessions and demands? Does it widen, or narrow, the actors' realm of tactical options? Does it open the way for agreement on a formula or end a stalemate over a particularly troublesome detail?

IMPLICATIONS FOR NEGOTIATION PRACTITIONERS

What do these findings imply about how negotiators should behave when involved in an asymmetrical negotiation? Below, we offer some specific guidelines for strong and for weak negotiators. But both the strong and the weak should keep three points in mind.

First, neither side should assume that the state with greater aggregate structural power will win the negotiation. Many negotiation theorists have made this mistake, as we discussed in chapter 2. The weak must not lose hope or become discouraged by even a glaring asymmetry. The strong must not become overconfident or assume that the weak state has no ability to achieve at least some of its objectives.

The second, and related, point is that both weak and strong should constantly try to assess the components of the issue power balance—alternatives, commitment, and control. Negotiators must be able to assess the issue power balance at any given point in the negotiations as well as try to understand to what degree and to whose favor the balance is changing. Doing so will help them choose from among their various tactical options and decide the most appropriate moment to use particular tactics. For example, if it appears that the issue power balance is changing in favor of the weak state, the strong state will want to pursue tactics that increase its issue power. Or, if such tactics prove unsuccessful, it may choose to use its tactical power to bring the negotiations to a rapid close, so as to preserve as much of its gains as possible. The weak state, on the other hand, should pursue tactics that maintain and increase its favorable issue power position.

There is no guarantee that both negotiators will have the same perception of the issue power balance. Differing perceptions can produce a crisis in the negotiations. Richard Nixon's perception of a favorable issue power balance in the Canal negotiations encouraged him to adopt a hard-line formula proposal in 1971. The formula backfired because Torrijos correctly perceived that the issue power balance was in fact shifting in Panama's favor; he thus strongly resisted Nixon's tactic. Franco also miscalculated the issue power balance in the 1951–53 bases negotiations, causing him to make demands the United States was unwilling to concede.

Because miscalculating the issue power balance is likely to cause a crisis in negotiations, both actors must focus on their respective issue power positions. Placing too much emphasis on the aggregate structural power balance can cause negotiators to overlook what is, in negotiation, the more important dimension of power.

Finally, both actors should be aware of the systemic and contextual factors and use them to their utmost advantage. Understanding the context will help negotiators determine the right moment for pursuing a particular tactic, whether it be causing a crisis, making a demand, or offering a concession. It will also help them determine what their range of tactics is. For example, in the global context of the early and mid-1970s, coercion was not a tactic the United States could consider using against Panama.

Learning to exploit contextual and systemic factors is especially critical for the weak state, since such factors often serve as constraints on the strong state's behavior. Riding favorable historical waves also bolsters the weak state's commitment, enhances its persuasive ability, and facilitates tactics such as coalition building. The tactical behavior of

Panama's Torrijos, who had an uncanny ability to exploit contextual changes, should serve as a guide for all weak states.

Strategies for the Strong

The principal lesson for the strong state is that its strength may not easily be translated into a negotiation "victory." Nevertheless, its strength, in the form of structural power resources, is real, and the advantages that accrue from it should not be overlooked. Thus, the first and most obvious element of a strong state's strategy is to be aware of the advantages its structural power gives it, such as a larger realm of tactical options, and to use those advantages within the limits posed by existing constraints.

The strong state should be equally aware of the weak state's advantages and learn to predict and even preempt the weak state's tactics. The United States, for example, was surprised and shocked by the pro-Panamanian outcome of the Security Council meeting in Panama City. Yet had American negotiators paid closer attention to Torrijos's tactics of coalition building, as well as to the growing anti-imperialist sentiment in the Third World, they might have been willing to make concessions that would have forestalled the unprecedented U.N. meeting. They would have certainly been better prepared for its outcome. Similarly, had the British realized that Iceland possessed few available tactics other than harassing the British fleet, they might have had second thoughts about provoking encounters that resulted only in greater international sympathy for the Icelanders.

As noted earlier, the weak state is likely to have an advantage in the commitment component of issue power. The strong state should thus consider ways to compensate for, if not reduce, the weak state's commitment. For example, the strong state may try to develop its alternatives, a tactic made possible by its great aggregate structural power. When the United States explored the option of building a new Central American canal, Panamanian commitment to its desired outcome noticeably declined.

Our findings also suggest some more specific elements of strategy for a strong state. For example, it may wish to appease the weak state by conceding on issues of principle and justice. Often the weak state's primary objective in negotiations with a strong state is the righting of a perceived wrong. For example, Panama felt that it should have sovereignty over the Canal; Spain wanted to be treated on an equal basis with America's other allies; and Iceland believed it had sovereign rights over its only natural resource. When possible, the strong state should concede on issues of principle. Doing so can benefit the strong state in two ways.

First, these concessions will often be largely symbolic. Yet they are concessions nonetheless, and negotiation norms call on the weak state to respond with concessions of its own. Britain, for example, could have acknowledged Iceland's expanded jurisdiction over territorial waters early in the Cod War negotiations and then attempted to elicit corresponding concessions on fishing rights. Instead, the British went for all or nothing and got nothing.

Second, conceding on issues of principle hinders the weak state's ability to form coalitions (which often are based on shared principles) and weakens its commitment. It was easy for Torrijos to arouse the Panamanian people over the question of sovereignty. But once the United States acknowledged Panamanian sovereignty, it became harder for Torrijos to rally Panamanians around the more substantive questions of defense rights and treaty duration.

Therefore the strong state should get tough on questions of detail. If the strong state concedes on symbolic points, usually embodied in the formula, it is in a better position to make tough demands on details, as the United States did in the Canal negotiations. After granting Panama the sovereignty issue in the Kissinger-Tack formula, the United States fought for, and won, significant concessions from Panama on defense rights.

Getting tough on details makes sense for another reason as well. The strong state, by definition, has greater aggregate structural power resources. These resources allow for such tactics as side payments, rewards, and threats to withhold earlier concessions—all of which are more likely to be effective in the detail phase. The detail phase resembles horse-trading, and in horse-trading, the more horses you have, the better you will do.

Strategies for the Weak

The principal lesson for the weak state is that despite its weakness it may still achieve many, even most, of its objectives. But to succeed, it must be aware of its strengths and advantages. Our findings point to several generic advantages a weak state is likely to possess. We noted that proximity to the field of play can increase the weak state's control. The implication is that weak states should pick their fights carefully. This advantage generally takes care of itself, since weak states' interests are usually confined to a small and proximate geographic area. They are unlikely to be involved in negotiations over matters far from home (though there are exceptions, such as trade negotiations, which are not geographically confined).

As noted, commitment is the most important component of issue power for the weak actor. It is therefore vital that the weak actor ensures that its commitment, both of its leadership and its domestic constituency, never wanes. Strong commitment facilitates tactics such as coalition building and the making of threats. The commitment component of issue power is the one most likely to be in the weak state's favor. Maintaining and strengthening one's natural advantages are the most effective means of achieving objectives.

In addition to tactics that are based on and strengthen commitment, the weak state should consider those other tactics which our findings and case studies indicate may be effective. These include coalition building, the threat to veto negotiations, and, if the situation allows, threats and even actual violence. None of these tactics derives from structural power resources; they derive instead from a favorable issue power balance and the creative use of behavioral power.

Another tactical element a weak state may use is to cause or threaten to cause crises. One of the biggest problems the weak have in negotiating with the strong is getting, and keeping, the opponent's attention. One way to do so is to cause periodic crises. Oran Young describes why causing crises is a useful tactic for weak states: "Because crises are relatively short, coercive, dangerous, and characterized by uncertainty, the importance of superior will and resolve tends to rise significantly in comparison with that of possessing superior capabilities in any physical sense."[3]

Crises are especially effective in the diagnostic phase, since they color the way the conflict is perceived and defined. The 1964 riots in Panama affected American perceptions of the Canal conflict for the next thirteen years. Crises may also prove useful in other phases of the negotiation process, as a means of keeping the strong state from backtracking, of resisting threats or coercion, and of ensuring that the issue does not drift too far off the strong state's agenda. In addition, crises may bring about a favorable change in the issue power balance by giving the perception that the weak state's control has increased.

There is a caveat, however. Causing a crisis is not a risk-free tactic. A crisis may provoke the strong state into responding coercively, and therefore could bring the negotiations to a quick end. Furthermore, negotiations arising from a crisis tend to focus on terminating the immediate confrontation rather than on resolving underlying problems.[4] Panama faced this dilemma in the immediate aftermath of the 1964 riots. The Johnson administration placed priority on normalizing U.S.-Panamanian relations, and not on addressing the sovereignty issue.

Thus, the tactic of causing crises should be used with caution. The weak state must know just how far it can push the strong state and must make sure that the ensuing negotiations focus on the real issues.

Finally, the weak state may try to include as many details as possible in the formula. It was suggested above that the strong state follow a tactic of conceding on symbolic issues in the formula phase, then adopting a harder line in the detail phase, in which its aggregate structural power can be used more effectively. To counteract this tactic, the weak state should try to work as many details as possible into the formula; in other words, not to let the strong state get away with making purely symbolic concessions, however important these may be. Iceland was very successful at this. In the Cod War negotiations, the formula and detail phases were virtually one and the same. Panama, on the other hand, might have fared better had it been able to include more substantive details in the Kissinger-Tack formula.

IMPLICATIONS FOR INTERNATIONAL RELATIONS THEORY

The framework of power developed in this study has important implications for international relations theory. Although our focus has been on negotiation, and more specifically, asymmetrical negotiation, much of what was revealed about power may contribute to a better understanding of other forms of interstate interaction as well.

Our findings build upon and support the work of political scientists and international relations theorists such as Stanley Hoffmann, David Baldwin, Joseph Nye, and Robert Keohane, who have challenged the premises and assumptions of conventional theories of power. Negotiation outcomes are not dependent solely, or even primarily, upon aggregate structural power resources. These resources are not always easily translated into behavioral power.

More important, we cannot view power as an all-encompassing concept. Instead, we must begin to look at power as a multidimensional concept: the power of aggregate resources, the power of issue-specific resources, and the power of tactics and human behavior. An asymmetry in any one of these dimensions of power can offset an asymmetry in any other. An undue focus on the aggregate dimension alone will render us less able to address asymmetries in the other dimensions and leave us baffled by unexpected outcomes. In addition, our findings endorse the view of power as a dynamic causal process rather than a static measure of capability. That is, the concept of power cannot be divorced from behavior and outcome.

These observations do not mean that we have entered a new world in which aggregate power resources are irrelevant and the weak have inherited the earth. Aggregate power is still important in international relations. But it must be seen as only one dimension of power which, although it affects and interacts with the other dimensions, does not necessarily predominate in the determination of outcomes.

This study has particular limitations. First, our analysis and findings were limited to asymmetrical negotiation, which is only one type of international interaction. Other types of interaction between weak and strong, such as open warfare or trade patterns, have different dynamics with which our framework of power may not be compatible. Second, we were dealing with cases in which the protagonists were friends, if not allies. This fact produced certain characteristics that will not apply in all cases. For example, it imposed restraints on the strong state's ability to behave more coercively. It is doubtful that negotiations between the United States and Cuba would follow the same relatively peaceful course as the Canal negotiations. Third, in each of our cases the strong state was a liberal, Western democracy. This factor also served as a restraint on using coercive tactics. Cases in which the strong state is governed by a totalitarian or authoritarian regime, or is composed of a society that does not share Western values and norms, are not likely to resemble the ones we studied. The Soviet Union's "negotiations" with the Dubçek regime in Czechoslovakia (an ally, no less) provides a sobering example.

In sum, when using the framework of power developed in this study, we should heed the warning of Hedley Bull: "The very intellectual completeness and logical tidiness of the model-building operation lends it an air of authority which is often quite misleading as to its standing as a statement about the real world."[5] To ensure the framework's usefulness as an analytical tool we must conduct many more case studies of asymmetrical negotiation and pay rigorous attention to the unique characteristics of each case. If the analysis seems to diverge from the framework, it is the framework that should give way. Frameworks are created to guide analysis and to assist in organizing data. But true understanding comes only from examining the often tortuous course negotiations take.

Nevertheless, within the parameters of our case studies, parameters that encompass many international negotiations, the findings of this study present important conclusions for analysts of negotiation, asymmetry, and power.

Notes

CHAPTER ONE INTRODUCTION:
ASYMMETRICAL NEGOTIATION

1. See Zartman, *The 50% Solution*, pp. 2–41, for a discussion of negotiation as a decision-making mechanism.

2. Young, *Bargaining*, p. 303.

3. Hoffmann, "Choices," pp. 3–42.

4. Morse, *Modernization and the Transformation of International Relations*, p. 46.

5. See Hopmann, "Asymmetrical Bargaining in the Conference on Security and Cooperation in Europe," pp. 141–77. Hopmann argues that "theories of negotiation [must] include assumptions about the effects of structural asymmetry upon the bargaining process" (p. 143).

6. Iklé, *How Nations Negotiate*.

7. Lall, *Modern International Negotiations*, p. 136.

8. Rubin and Brown, *The Social Psychology of Bargaining and Negotiation*, p. 199.

9. Lockhart, *Bargaining in International Conflicts*, p. 92.

10. Snyder and Diesing, *Conflict among Nations*, p. 190.

11. Barston, "The External Relations of Small States," in *Small States in International Relations*, ed. Schou and Brundtland, p. 46.

12. Bjol, "The Small State in International Politics," in *Small States in International Relations*, ed. Schou and Brundtland, p. 36. See also Aron, *Peace and War*.

13. Fox, *The Power of Small States*, and idem, *The Politics of Attraction*.

14. Vital, "The Analysis of Small Power Politics," in *Small States in International Relations*, ed. Schou and Brundtland, pp. 15–27.

15. Hopmann, "Asymmetrical Bargaining."

16. Odell, "Latin American Trade Negotiations with the United States," pp. 207–28.

17. Odell, "The Outcome of International Trade Conflicts," pp. 263–86.

18. Wriggins, "Up for Auction," in *The 50% Solution*, ed. Zartman, pp. 208–34.

19. Dobell, "Negotiating with the United States," pp. 17–69.

20. Robert L. Rothstein, *Global Bargaining*.

21. Zartman, *The Politics of Trade Negotiations between Africa and the European Economic Community*, p. 5.
22. Zartman, "The Political Analysis of Negotiation," p. 394.

CHAPTER TWO POWER AND NEGOTIATION

1. Zartman, *The 50% Solution*, p. 15.
2. Claude, *Power and International Relations*, p. 6.
3. Morgenthau, *Politics among Nations*, p. 39.
4. Schelling, *The Strategy of Conflict;* Rapoport, *Fights, Games, and Debates;* and Von Neumann and Morgenstern, *Theory of Games and Economic Behavior.*
5. See Nash, "The Bargaining Problem," pp. 155–62.
6. Cross, *The Economics of Bargaining,* and "Negotiation as a Learning Process," pp. 581–606; Bartos, *Process and Outcome of Negotiations,* and "Simple Model of Negotiation," pp. 565–79; and Contini, "The Value of Time in Bargaining Negotiations," pp. 374–93.
7. Zeuthen, *Problems of Monopoly and Economic Warfare;* Pen, "A General Theory of Bargaining," pp. 24–42; and Hicks, *The Theory of Wages.*
8. Bartos, "Simple Model of Negotiation."
9. de Callières, *On the Manner of Negotiating with Princes;* and Nicolson, *Diplomacy.*
10. Deutsch, *The Resolution of Conflict;* and Rubin and Brown, *The Social Psychology of Bargaining and Negotiation.*
11. Snyder and Diesing, *Conflict among Nations,* p. 308.
12. Rubin and Brown, *The Social Psychology of Bargaining and Negotiation,* passim.
13. Spector, "Negotiation as a Psychological Process," in *The Negotiation Process,* ed. Zartman, pp. 55–56. For a good overview of the psychological literature, see Hermann and Kogan, "Effects of Negotiators' Personalities on Negotiating Behavior," in *Negotiations,* ed. Druckman.
14. Zartman, "Negotiation as a Joint Decision-Making Process," in *The Negotiation Process,* ed. Zartman, p. 72.
15. See Bell, Edwards, and Wagner, *Political Power;* and Dahl, "Power," in *International Encyclopedia of the Social Sciences,* vol. 12, pp. 405–15.
16. Robert Dahl's definition of power suffers from a similar problem of tautology. Dahl, who uses the terms *power* and *influence* interchangeably, writes: "A influences B to the extent that he changes B's actions or predispositions in some way" (p. 29). This statement helps us to recognize when power has occurred in a relationship, but it does not define power. Dahl, *Modern Political Analysis.*
17. This definition of power derives in part from the influence of a number of political theorists, including Dahl (the criticism in note 16 notwithstanding), Harold Lasswell and Abraham Kaplan, Bertrand Russell, and Jack Nagel. Lasswell and Kaplan define power as "the process of affecting policies of others with the help of (actual or threatened) severe deprivations for nonconformity" (*Power and Society,* p. 76). Bertrand Russell succinctly defines power as "the production of

intended effects," thus emphasizing the dynamic, processual nature of power (*Power*, p. 35). Nagel's contribution is his emphasis on the causal nature of a power relationship: "A power relation, actual or potential, is an actual or potential causal relation between the preferences of an actor regarding an outcome and the outcome itself" (*The Descriptive Analysis of Power*, p. 29).

18. For a lucid discussion of this debate, see Nagel, *The Descriptive Analysis of Power*.

19. Ibid., p. 24.

20. Steven Lukes illuminates this point by noting the difference between "power to," a facility or an ability, and "power over," which indicates a relationship (*Power*, p. 31.)

21. Cline, *World Power Assessment*, p. 11.

22. Jones, "The Power Inventory and National Strategy," p. 421.

23. Cline, *World Power Trends and U.S. Foreign Policy for the 1980s*, p. 22. Although Cline's formula has an aura of scientific infallibility, the numbers used to weigh and quantify its elements are, in his own words, "subjective and, in a sense, arbitrary judgments" (p. 23).

24. Waltz, *Theory of International Politics*, pp. 131, 192.

25. Baldwin, "Power Analysis and World Politics," p. 192.

26. Ibid., p. 165. See also Goldmann, "The International Power Structure," in *Power, Capabilities, and Interdependence*, ed. Goldmann and Sjostedt, pp. 7–36; Hart, "Three Approaches to the Measurement of Power in International Relations," pp. 289–305; Hoffmann, "Notes on the Elusiveness of Modern Power," pp. 183–206; Sprout and Sprout, *The Ecological Perspective on Human Affairs*, and *Toward a Politics of the Planet Earth*.

27. Keohane and Nye, *Power and Interdependence*, p. 8.

28. McClintock, Steach, and Keil, "The Influence of Communication upon Bargaining," in *Basic Group Processes*, ed. Paul B. Paulus, pp. 205–33.

29. Kenneth Waltz notwithstanding. Waltz defines interdependence as a relationship of near equality: "Two or more parties are interdependent if they depend on one another about equally for the supply of goods and services. They are interdependent if the costs of breaking their relations or of reducing their exchanges are about equal for both of them" (*Theory of International Politics*, p. 143). The view of interdependence as relationships of equal costs is subject to challenge. Interdependent relationships develop between states because the costs of *not* being in that relationship are too great. This proposition does not imply that the costs to each actor are equally great. For a more thorough critique of Waltz's view, see Baldwin, "Interdependence and Power," pp. 471–506.

30. Keohane and Nye, *Power and Interdependence*, p. 11.

31. Ibid., p. 50.

32. McClintock et al., "The Influence of Communication upon Bargaining," p. 207. For the fundamentals of social exchange theory, see Blau, *Exchange and Power in Social Life*; Homans, *Social Behavior*; and Thibaut and Kelley, *The Social Psychology of Groups*.

33. Emerson, "Power-Dependence Relations," pp. 31–41.

34. Thibaut and Kelley, *The Social Psychology of Groups*.

35. Keohane and Nye, *Power and Interdependence,* p. 18.
36. Jönsson, "Bargaining Power," pp. 249–57, quotation on p. 252.
37. Ibid.

CHAPTER THREE THE NEGOTIATION PROCESS

1. Iklé, *How Nations Negotiate,* esp. chap. 11.
2. Rubin and Brown, *The Social Psychology of Bargaining and Negotiation,* p. 14.
3. Raiffa, *The Art and Science of Negotiation,* p. 128.
4. Bartos, "Simple Model of Negotiation," in *The Negotiation Process,* ed. Zartman, pp. 13–27.
5. Cross, "Negotiation as a Learning Process," in *The Negotiation Process,* ed. Zartman, p. 29.
6. Zartman, "Negotiation as a Joint Decision-Making Process," in *The Negotiation Process,* ed. Zartman, p. 81; and Zartman and Berman, *The Practical Negotiator,* pp. xi–xiii.
7. Zartman, "Negotiation as a Joint Decision-Making Process," p. 76.
8. Zartman and Berman, *The Practical Negotiator,* p. 54.
9. Druckman, "Stages, Turning Points, and Crises," p. 6.

CHAPTER FOUR THE PANAMA CANAL NEGOTIATIONS

1. For a good discussion of the history of the 1903 treaty, see LaFeber, *The Panama Canal.*
2. The text of the 1903 treaty can be found in Malloy, ed., *Treaties, Conventions, International Acts, Protocols, and Agreements between the United States of America and Other Powers, 1776–1909,* vol. 2, pp. 1349–57.
3. For an account of the events occurring between September 1977 and June 1978, see Jorden, *Panama Odyssey,* pp. 457–626. Also useful are the memoirs of the major participants: Jimmy Carter, *Keeping Faith;* Cyrus R. Vance, *Hard Choices;* Zbigniew Brzezinski, *Power and Principle;* and Sol M. Linowitz, *The Making of a Public Man.*
4. Jorden, *Panama Odyssey,* p. 24.
5. Farnsworth and McKenney, *U.S.-Panama Relations, 1903–1978,* p. 90.
6. See Leopold, *The Growth of American Foreign Policy,* chaps. 20, 36.
7. LaFeber, *The Panama Canal,* pp. 132–36.
8. Ibid., p. 136.
9. For an excellent discussion of the Canal Zone's legal status, see Shay, "The Panama Canal Zone," pp. 15–60.
10. See particularly Jorden, *Panama Odyssey,* chap. 3.
11. *New York Times,* January 12, 1964.
12. Ibid., January 11, 1964.
13. Ibid., January 12, 1964.
14. Jorden, *Panama Odyssey,* p. 30.

15. Ibid., p. 71.

16. *New York Times,* January 24, 1964.

17. Ibid., January 26, 1964.

18. Ibid., March 1, 1964.

19. Ibid., March 22, 1964.

20. Ibid., April 4, 1964.

21. Ibid.

22. Ibid. Emphasis added.

23. Johnson, *The Vantage Point,* p. 183.

24. Scranton, "Changing United States Foreign Policy," p. 224.

25. Jorden, *Panama Odyssey,* p. 95.

26. *New York Times,* April 17, 1964.

27. Jorden, *Panama Odyssey,* p. 95.

28. *New York Times,* May 5, 1964.

29. Jorden, *Panama Odyssey,* p. 100.

30. *New York Times,* December 19, 1964.

31. Zartman and Berman, *The Practical Negotiator,* pp. 87-88.

32. *New York Times,* December 27, 1964.

33. Ibid., December 20, 1964.

34. Jorden, *Panama Odyssey,* p. 107.

35. *U.S. News and World Report,* December 4, 1965, p. 6.

36. *New York Times,* December 11, 1966.

37. Jorden, *Panama Odyssey,* p. 117.

38. *New York Times,* September 10, 1967.

39. *New York Times,* September 14, 1967.

40. LaFeber, *The Panama Canal,* p. 147.

41. I. William Zartman, "Ripening Conflict, Ripe Moment, Formula and Mediation," in *Perspectives on Negotiation,* ed. Diane B. Bendahmane and John W. McDonald, Jr., p. 210.

42. Jorden, *Panama Odyssey,* pp. 101-2.

43. *New York Times,* September 2, 1969.

44. Ibid.

45. Ibid., September 3, 1970.

46. Atlantic-Pacific Interoceanic Canal Study Commission, *Interoceanic Canal Studies, 1970,* pp. 108-9.

47. LaFeber, *The Panama Canal,* p. 184.

48. Jorden, *Panama Odyssey,* p. 161.

49. Scranton, "Changing United States Foreign Policy," p. 321.

50. Zartman and Berman, *The Practical Negotiator,* p. 109.

51. Jorden, *Panama Odyssey,* pp. 161-62.

52. *New York Times,* October 12, 1972.

53. Thomas Schelling discusses this tactic in *The Strategy of Conflict,* pp. 123-24.

54. *New York Times,* October 19, 1971.

55. Jorden, *Panama Odyssey,* p. 155.

56. United States Congress, House of Representatives, Subcommittee on Inter-

American Affairs of the Committee on Foreign Affairs, *Panama Canal, 1971.*
Typical of the statements made during these hearings was that of Congressman
Daniel Flood: "No wonder the eyes of the world are watching us at Panama, for on
what we do there could well depend the freedom or slavery of the world" (p. 11).

57. Jorden, *Panama Odyssey,* p. 173.

58. *New York Times,* November 12, 1972.

59. Ibid., March 15, 16, and 22, 1973.

60. Jorden, *Panama Odyssey,* p. 198.

61. Rosenfeld, "The Panama Negotiations," p. 4.

62. United States Congress, House of Representatives, Committee on Merchant Marine and Fisheries, *Briefings Concerning Treaty Negotiations and Current Activities of the Panama Canal and Canal Zone,* p. 12.

63. United States Congress, House of Representatives, Committee on Foreign Affairs and Committee on Merchant Marine and Fisheries, *United Nations Security Council Meeting in Panama,* p. 11.

64. Ibid., p. 17.

65. Scranton, "Changing United States Foreign Policy," p. 391.

66. Furlong and Scranton, *The Dynamics of Foreign Policy Making,* p. 49.

67. Nixon, "Fourth Annual Report to the Congress on United States Foreign Policy, May 3, 1973," in *Public Papers of the Presidents of the United States: Richard Nixon, 1978,* p. 443.

68. Quoted in Jorden, *Panama Odyssey,* p. 176, emphasis in original.

69. Ibid., p. 204.

70. Linowitz, *The Making of a Public Man,* p. 146.

71. Interview with American participant.

72. Jorden, *Panama Odyssey,* p. 696.

73. Ibid., p. 221.

74. *New York Times,* March 30, 1974.

75. Ibid., February 4, 1975.

76. LaFeber, *The Panama Canal,* p. 187.

77. Ibid., p. 189.

78. *New York Times,* July 28, 1975.

79. Ibid., September 24, 1975.

80. Ibid., March 15, 1976.

81. Quoted in LaFeber, *The Panama Canal,* p. 192.

82. *New York Times,* June 13, 1976.

83. Ibid., August 18, 1976.

84. Jorden, *Panama Odyssey,* p. 341.

85. Carter, *Keeping Faith,* p. 155. See also Vance, *Hard Choices,* p. 141.

86. Carter, *Keeping Faith,* p. 156. Carter's description of Panama as a "relatively defenseless" nation contradicts his fears of a Panamanian assault on the Canal.

87. Commission on United States–Latin American Relations, *The Americas in a Changing World.*

88. Brzezinski, *Power and Principle,* p. 136. Secretary of State Vance shared this view; see Vance, *Hard Choices,* p. 145.

89. *New York Times,* January 31, 1977.

90. Ibid., March 6, 1977.

91. Scranton, "Changing United States Foreign Policy," p. 437.

92. Zartman and Berman, *The Practical Negotiator,* p. 189.

93. LaFeber, *The Panama Canal,* pp. 205–6.

94. For the full text of the treaty, see *Department of State Bulletin,* October 17, 1977, pp. 483–502.

95. See Iklé, *How Nations Negotiate,* pp. 30–35.

96. United States Congress, Senate, Committee on Foreign Relations, *Senate Debate on the Panama Canal Treaties,* p. 20.

97. Ibid., p. 174.

98. For a valuable discussion of the political context, see Furlong and Scranton, *The Dynamics of Foreign Policy Making.*

99. Interview with American participant.

CHAPTER FIVE   U.S.–SPANISH BASES NEGOTIATIONS

1. Lowi, *Bases in Spain,* p. 3.

2. "U.S. Policy toward Spain," NSC-3, 1947, in *Foreign Relations of the United States, 1947,* vol. 2: *The British Commonwealth; Europe,* pp. 1092–95.

3. For the military arguments for an improved relationship with Spain, see Fernsworth, "Spain in Western Defense," pp. 648–62; and a two-part article on Spain in the *London Times,* August 20 and 21, 1951.

4. Lowi, *Bases in Spain,* p. 17.

5. Ibid., p. 10.

6. For discussions of the important ramifications of NSC-68 on U.S. foreign policy, see Gaddis, *Strategies of Containment;* and Wells, "Sounding the Tocsin, pp. 116–38.

7. The untitled memorandum appears in *Foreign Relations of the United States, 1950,* vol. 3: *Western Europe,* pp. 1560–62.

8. "Views of the Department of State on United States Policy toward Spain," July 3, 1950, in *Foreign Relations of the United States, 1950,* vol. 3: *Western Europe,* pp. 1570–72.

9. Weeks, "United States Defense Policy toward Spain, 1950–1976," p. 85.

10. *New York Times,* July 18, 1951. The memorandum of Admiral Sherman's meeting with Franco has yet to be declassified.

11. Ibid., March 19, 1951.

12. Ibid., June 8, 1951.

13. Ibid., July 29, 1951, and August 12, 1951.

14. Ibid., July 20, 1951.

15. Ibid., January 26, 1952.

16. Ibid.

17. Ibid., March 13, 1952.

18. Ibid., April 1, 1952.

19. Ibid., April 16, 1952.

20. Franco's memorandum is discussed in a Department of State Review Memorandum, "Status Report on Spanish Negotiations," October 6, 1952.

21. *New York Times,* July 29, 1952.

22. Ibid., August 1952, passim.

23. Department of State Review Memorandum, "Status Report on Spanish Negotiations," October 6, 1952.

24. Whitaker, *Spain and Defense of the West,* pp. 44–48.

25. Rubottom and Murphy, *Spain and the United States,* p. 78.

26. *New York Times,* September 27, 1963.

27. Ibid., November 10, 1968.

28. Ibid., August 11, 1968.

29. Ibid., September 28, 1968.

30. Ibid.

31. Ibid.

32. Ibid., November 8, 1968.

33. Ibid., November 10, 1968.

34. Weeks, "United States Defense Policy toward Spain, 1950–1976," p. 191.

35. See Tracy, "Bargaining as Trial and Error," in *The Negotiation Process,* ed. Zartman, pp. 193–224.

36. *New York Times,* March 23, 1969.

37. Tracy, "Bargaining as Trial and Error," in *The Negotiation Process,* ed. Zartman, p. 210.

38. *New York Times,* March 23, 1969. Note that the Pentagon's position on Spanish bases contradicted that of the National Security Council.

39. Story, "Spanish Foreign Policy, 1945–1970," p. 178.

40. *New York Times,* June 22, 1969.

41. Weeks, "United States Defense Policy toward Spain, 1950–1976," p. 200.

42. *New York Times,* May 28, 1970.

43. Ibid., May 30, 1970.

44. Ibid., June 21, 1970.

45. Ibid., July 25, 1970.

46. Ibid., August 7, 1970.

47. Weeks, "United States Defense Policy toward Spain, 1950–1976," p. 244.

48. King, "On Quitting Spain," p. 29.

49. *New York Times,* September 24, 1975.

50. Weeks, "United States Defense Policy toward Spain, 1950–1976," p. 267.

51. Ibid., p. 271.

52. *New York Times,* October 5, 1975.

53. Weeks, "United States Defense Policy toward Spain, 1950–1967," p. 272.

54. Jerry Strickland presents this argument in "Treaty with Spain," pp. 852–56.

CHAPTER SIX THE ANGLO-ICELANDIC COD WARS

1. See, for example, the Icelandic Law of 1948, in Jónsson, *Friends in Conflict,* pp. 52–54.

2. Ibid., p. 58.

3. Ibid., pp. 7, 211.

4. Ibid., p. 209.

5. Ibid., p. 74.

6. *Keesings Contemporary Archives,* Bristol: Keesings Publications, Ltd., November 1–8, 1958, p. 16478.

7. Jónsson, *Friends in Conflict,* p. 2.

8. *Keesings,* November 1–8, 1958, p. 16478.

9. Report on the British Fishing Industry Distant Water Trawlers, "Fishing in Distant Waters," pp. 22–24.

10. Jónsson, *Friends in Conflict,* p. 88.

11. Griffiths, *Modern Iceland,* p. 130.

12. Gilchrist, *Cod Wars and How to Lose Them,* p. 68.

13. Ibid., p. 70.

14. Ibid. Emphasis in original.

15. Quoted in ibid, p. 74.

16. Ibid., p. 75.

17. Zartman and Berman, *The Practical Negotiator,* p. 87.

18. *Keesings,* November 1–8, 1958, p. 16479.

19. Ibid.

20. Jónsson, *Friends in Conflict,* p. 74.

21. *Keesings,* November 1–8, 1958, p. 16480.

22. Ibid., June 11–18, 1960, p. 17476.

23. *London Times,* July 1, 1959.

24. Gilchrist, *Cod Wars and How to Lose Them,* p. 97.

25. The letter is reproduced in Jónsson, *Friends in Conflict,* p. 101.

26. Ibid., p. 102.

27. Ibid., pp. 103–4.

28. Quoted in ibid., p. 126.

29. The Vienna Convention is discussed in Bishop, *International Law,* pp. 121–22.

30. *Hansard's Parliamentary Debates,* 5th ser., House of Commons, vol. 821, col. 1416.

31. Jónsson, *Friends in Conflict,* p. 5.

32. Ibid., pp. 209, 211.

33. Ibid., p. 140.

34. *Keesings,* April 29–May 6, 1972, p. 25235.

35. Speech by Baroness Tweedsmuir before Parliament, March 2, 1972. *Hansard's Parliamentary Debates,* 5th ser., House of Lords, vol. 328, cols. 1257–63.

36. Ibid., vol. 832, col. 1007.

37. *Keesings,* April 29–May 6, 1972, pp. 25235–36.

38. Ibid., pp. 25869, 25871.

39. Statement by Sir Anthony Royle before Parliament, October 19, 1972. *Hansard's Parliamentary Debates,* 5th ser., House of Commons, vol. 843, cols. 458–62.

40. *Keesings,* May 7–13, 1973, p. 25873.

41. Ibid.

42. Statement by Sir Alec Douglas-Home before Parliament, November 30, 1972. *Hansard's Parliamentary Debates,* 5th ser., House of Commons, vol. 847, cols. 636–43.

43. *Hansard's Partliamentary Debates,* 5th ser., House of Commons, vol. 849, col. 37.

44. *Keesings,* August 6–12, 1973, p. 26028.

45. Ibid., p. 26029.

46. Ibid.

47. Jónsson, *Friends in Conflict,* p. 140.

48. Quoted in the *Manchester Guardian,* May 29, 1973.

49. See Mitchell, "Politics, Fish, and International Resource Management," p. 128.

50. "Fisheries Dispute between the United Kingdom and Iceland," cmnd. 5341.

51. Jónsson, *Friends in Conflict,* p. 150.

52. *Keesings,* December 10–16, 1973, p. 26238.

53. *Cod War III between Iceland and Great Britain,* pp. 17, 19, 28.

54. Ibid., p. 26.

55. *The Fishery Limits off Iceland,* p. 36.

56. Jónsson, *Friends in Conflict,* p. 159.

57. *Keesings,* January 9, 1976, p. 27514.

58. Ibid., p. 27515.

59. Ibid., p. 27511.

60. Ibid., p. 27513.

61. Ibid., March 26, 1976, p. 27637.

62. Jónsson, *Friends in Conflict,* p. 175.

63. Ibid., p. 177.

64. For an expanded discussion of Keflavik's importance to NATO, see Sparring, "Iceland, Europe, and NATO," pp. 393–403.

65. Jónsson, *Friends in Conflict,* p. 164.

66. *Keesings,* July 9, 1976, p. 27825.

67. Ibid., p. 27824.

68. *Hansard's Parliamentary Debates,* 5th ser., House of Commons, vol. 912, col. 936.

69. *Keesings,* July 9, 1976, p. 27824.

CHAPTER SEVEN CONCLUSIONS:
FINDINGS AND IMPLICATIONS

1. Oran Young terms this "logistical asymmetry" and notes that it can counterbalance other asymmetries between the actors. Young, *The Politics of Force,* p. 216.

2. Nye, "Transnational Relations and Interstate Conflicts," p. 992.

3. Young, *The Politics of Force,* pp. 175–76.

4. Ibid., p. 285.

5. Bull, "International Theory," in *Contending Approaches to International Politics,* ed. Knorr and Rosenau, p. 31.

Bibliography

Aron, Raymond. *Peace and War: A Theory of International Relations*. Melbourne, Fla.: Krieger Press, 1981.

Atlantic-Pacific Interoceanic Canal Study Commission. *Interoceanic Canal Studies, 1970*. Washington, D.C.: G.P.O., 1971.

Baldwin, David A. "Interdependence and Power: A Conceptual Analysis." *International Organization* 34 (Autumn 1980): 471–506.

———"Power Analysis and World Politics: New Trends versus Old Tendencies." *World Politics* 31 (January 1979): 161–94.

Barston, Ronald P. "The External Relations of Small States." In *Small States in International Relations*, edited by August Schou and Arne Olav Brundtland. Stockholm: Almqvist & Wiskell, 1971.

Bartos, Otomar J. *Process and Outcome of Negotiations*. New York: Columbia University Press, 1974.

———"Simple Model of Negotiation: A Sociological Point of View." *Journal of Conflict Resolution* 21 (December 1977): 565–79.

Bell, Roderick, David V. Edwards, and R. Harrison Wagner. *Political Power: A Reader in Theory and Research*. New York: Free Press, 1969.

Bendahmane, Diane B., and John W. McDonald, Jr., eds. *Perspectives on Negotiation*. Washington, D.C.: G.P.O., 1986.

Bishop, William W., Jr. *International Law*. Boston: Little, Brown & Co., 1962.

Bjol, Erlin. "The Small State in International Politics." In *Small States in International Relations*, edited by August Schou and Arne Olav Brundtland. Stockholm: Almqvist & Wiskell, 1971.

Blau, Peter M. *Exchange and Power in Social Life*. New York: John Wiley & Sons, 1964.

Brzezinski, Zbigniew. *Power and Principle*. New York: Farrar, Straus, Giroux, 1983.

Bull, Hedley. "International Theory: The Case for a Classical Approach." In *Contending Approaches to International Politics*, edited by Klaus Knorr and James N. Rosenau. Princeton: Princeton University Press, 1969.

Carter, Jimmy. *Keeping Faith*. New York: Bantam Books, 1982.

Claude, Inis. *Power and International Relations*. New York: Random House, 1962.

Cline, Ray S. *World Power Assessment*. Washington, D.C.: Georgetown Center for Strategic and International Studies, 1975.

———— *World Power Trends and U.S. Foreign Policy for the 1980s*. Boulder, Colo.: Westview Press, 1980.

Cod War III between Iceland and Great Britain. Reykjavik: Government of Iceland, Ministry of Fisheries, December 1975.

Commission on United States-Latin American Relations. *The Americas in a Changing World*. New York: Quadrangle Press, 1975.

Contini, Bruno. "The Value of Time in Bargaining Negotiations: Some Experimental Evidence." *American Economic Review* 48 (June 1958): 374–93.

Cross, John G. *The Economics of Bargaining*. New York: Basic Books, 1969.

———— "Negotiation as a Learning Process." *Journal of Conflict Resolution* 21 (December 1977): 581–606.

Dahl, Robert A. *Modern Political Analysis*. Englewood Cliffs, N.J.: Prentice Hall, 1976.

———— "Power." In *International Encyclopedia of the Social Sciences*, vol. 12. New York: Crowell, Collier & Macmillan, 1968.

de Callières, François. *On the Manner of Negotiating with Princes*, translated by A. F. Whyte. Notre Dame, Ind.: University of Notre Dame Press, 1963.

Deutsch, Morton. *The Resolution of Conflict*. New Haven: Yale University Press, 1974.

Dobell, Peter C. "Negotiating with the United States." *International Journal* 36 (Winter 1980–81): 17–69.

Druckman, Daniel. "Stages, Turning Points, and Crises: Negotiating Military Base Rights, Spain and the United States." Manuscript, 1985.

————, ed. *Negotiations*. Beverly Hills: Sage, 1977.

Emerson, Richard. "Power-Dependence Relations." *American Sociological Review* 27 (February 1962): 31–41.

Farnsworth, David N., and James W. McKenney. *U.S.-Panama Relations, 1903–1978: A Study in Linkage Politics*. Boulder, Colo.: Westview Press, 1983.

Fernsworth, Lawrence. "Spain in Western Defense." *Foreign Affairs* (July 1953): 648–62.

"Fisheries Dispute between the United Kingdom and Iceland," cmnd. 5341. London: Her Majesty's Stationery Office, 1973.

The Fishery Limits off Iceland: 200 Nautical Miles. Reykjavik: Ministry for Foreign Affairs, January 1976.

"Fishing in Distant Waters." Report on the British Fishing Industry Distant Water Trawlers. Hull: Fleetwood, Grimsley, 1958.

Foreign Relations of the United States, 1947, vol. 2: *The British Commonwealth; Europe*. Washington, D.C.: G.P.O., 1972.

Foreign Relations of the United States, 1950, vol. 3: *Western Europe*. Washington, D.C.: G.P.O., 1977.

Fox, Annette Baker. *The Politics of Attraction*. New York: Columbia University Press, 1977.

———— *The Power of Small States*. Chicago: University of Chicago Press, 1959.

Furlong, William L., and Margaret E. Scranton. *The Dynamics of Foreign Policy Making*. Boulder, Colo.: Westview Press, 1984.

Gaddis, John Lewis. *Strategies of Containment*. New York: Oxford University Press, 1982.

Gilchrist, Sir Andrew. *Cod Wars and How to Lose Them*. Edinburgh: Q Press, 1978.

Goldmann, Kjell. "The International Power Structure." In *Power, Capabilities, and Interdependence*, edited by Kjell Goldmann and Gunnar Sjostedt. Beverly Hills: Sage, 1979.

Goldmann, Kjell, and Gunnar Sjostedt, eds. *Power, Capabilities, and Interdependence*. Beverly Hills: Sage, 1979.

Griffiths, John C. *Modern Iceland*. New York: Praeger, 1969.

Hart, Jeffrey. "Three Approaches to the Measurement of Power in International Relations." *International Organization* 30 (Spring 1976): 289–305.

Hermann, Margaret C., and Nathan Kogan. "Effects of Negotiators' Personalities on Negotiating Behavior." In *Negotiations*, edited by Daniel Druckman. Beverly Hills: Sage, 1977.

Hicks, J. R. *The Theory of Wages*. London: Macmillan, 1932.

Hoffmann, Stanley. "Choices." *Foreign Policy* 12 (Fall 1973): 3–42.

——— "Notes on the Elusiveness of Modern Power." *International Journal* 30 (Spring 1975): 183–206.

Homans, George. *Social Behavior*. New York: Harcourt, Brace, Jovanovich, 1961.

Hopmann, P. Terrence. "Asymmetrical Bargaining in the Conference on Security and Cooperation in Europe." *International Organization* 32 (Winter 1978): 141–77.

Iklé, Fred Charles. *How Nations Negotiate*. New York: Harper & Row, 1964.

Johnson, Lyndon B. *The Vantage Point*. New York: Holt, Rinehart & Winston, 1971.

Jones, Stephen B. "The Power Inventory and National Strategy." *World Politics* 6 (July 1954): 421–52.

Jönsson, Christer. "Bargaining Power: Notes on an Elusive Concept." *Cooperation and Conflict* 16 (December 1981): 249–57.

Jónsson, Hannes. *Friends in Conflict*. London: C. Hurst, 1982.

Jorden, William J. *Panama Odyssey*. Austin: University of Texas Press, 1984.

Keohane, Robert O., and Joseph S. Nye. *Power and Interdependence*. Boston: Little, Brown & Co., 1977.

King, Edward L. "On Quitting Spain." *New York Times,* September 20, 1975, p. 29.

Knorr, Klaus, and James N. Rosenau, eds. *Contending Approaches to International Politics*. Princeton: Princeton University Press, 1969.

LaFeber, Walter. *The Panama Canal*. New York: Oxford University Press, 1979.

Lall, Arthur. *Modern International Negotiations*. New York: Columbia University Press, 1966.

Lasswell, Harold D., and Abraham Kaplan. *Power and Society*. New Haven: Yale University Press, 1950.

Leopold, Richard W. *The Growth of American Foreign Policy*. New York: Knopf, 1962.

Linowitz, Sol M. *The Making of a Public Man.* Boston: Little, Brown & Co., 1985.
Lockhart, Charles. *Bargaining in International Conflicts.* New York: Columbia University Press, 1979.
Lowi, Theodore J. *Bases in Spain.* Indianapolis: Bobbs-Merrill, 1963.
Lukes, Steven. *Power: A Radical View.* New York: Macmillan, 1974.
McClintock, Charles G., Frank J. Steach, and Linda J. Keil. "The Influence of Communication upon Bargaining." In *Basic Group Processes,* edited by Paul B. Paulus. New York: Springer-Verlag, 1983.
Malloy, William M., ed. *Treaties, Conventions, International Acts, Protocols, and Agreements between the United States of America and Other Powers, 1776–1909,* vol. 2. Washington, D.C.: G.P.O., 1910.
Mitchell, Bruce. "Politics, Fish, and International Resource Management: The British Icelandic Cod War." *Geographical Review* 66 (April 1976): 127–38.
Morgenthau, Hans J. *Politics among Nations.* New York: Knopf, 1960.
Morse, Edward L. *Modernization and the Transformation of International Relations.* New York: Free Press, 1976.
Nagel, Jack H. *The Descriptive Analysis of Power.* New Haven: Yale University Press, 1975.
Nash, J. F. "The Bargaining Problem." *Econometrica* 18 (1950): 155–62.
Nicolson, Harold. *Diplomacy.* New York: Oxford University Press, 1964.
Nixon, Richard M. *Public Papers of the Presidents of the United States: Richard Nixon, 1978.* Washington, D.C.: G.P.O., 1975.
Nye, Joseph S. "Transnational Relations and Interstate Conflicts: An Empirical Analysis." *International Organization* 28 (Autumn 1974): 961–96.
Odell, John S. "Latin American Trade Negotiations with the United States." *International Organization* 34 (Spring 1980): 207–28.
——— "The Outcome of International Trade Conflicts: The U.S. and South Korea, 1960–1981." *International Studies Quarterly* 29 (September 1985): 263–86.
Paulus, Paul B., ed. *Basic Group Processes.* New York: Springer-Verlag, 1983.
Pen, John. "A General Theory of Bargaining." *American Economic Review* 42 (March 1952): 24–42.
Raiffa, Howard. *The Art and Science of Negotiation.* Cambridge: Harvard University Press, 1982.
Rapoport, Anatol. *Fights, Games, and Debates.* Ann Arbor: University of Michigan Press, 1960.
Rosenfeld, Stephen S. "The Panama Negotiations: A Close-Run Thing." *Foreign Affairs* 54 (October 1975): 1–13.
Rothstein, Robert L. *Global Bargaining: UNCTAD and the Quest for a New International Economic Order.* Princeton: Princeton University Press, 1977.
Rubin, Jeffrey Z., and Bert R. Brown. *The Social Psychology of Bargaining and Negotiation.* New York: Academic Press, 1975.
Rubottom, R. Richard, and J. Carter Murphy. *Spain and the United States.* New York: Praeger, 1984.
Russell, Bertrand. *Power.* New York: W. W. Norton, 1938.

Schelling, Thomas. *The Strategy of Conflict.* Cambridge: Harvard University Press, 1960.

Schou, August, and Arne Olav Brundtland. *Small States in International Relations.* Stockholm: Almqvist & Wiskell, 1971.

Scranton, Margaret E. "Changing United States Foreign Policy: Negotiating New Panama Canal Treaties, 1958–1978." Ph.D. dissertation, University of Pittsburgh, 1980.

Shay, Martha Jane. "The Panama Canal Zone: In Search of a Judicial Identity." *New York University Journal of International Law and Politics* 9 (Spring 1976): 15–60.

Snyder, Glenn H., and Paul Diesing. *Conflict among Nations.* Princeton: Princeton University Press, 1977.

Sparring, Ake. "Iceland, Europe, and NATO." *World Today* 28 (September 1972): 393–403.

Spector, Bertram. "Negotiation as a Psychological Process." In *The Negotiation Process,* edited by I. William Zartman. Beverly Hills: Sage, 1977.

Sprout, Harold, and Margaret Sprout. *The Ecological Perspective on Human Affairs.* Princeton: Princeton University Press, 1965.

——— *Toward a Politics of the Planet Earth.* New York: Van Nostrand Reinhold, 1971.

Story, Jonathan. "Spanish Foreign Policy, 1945–1970." Ph.D. dissertation, The Johns Hopkins University, 1973.

Strickland, Jerry. "Treaty with Spain." *Congressional Quarterly Weekly Report* 34 (April 10, 1976): 852–56.

Thibaut, John W., and Harold H. Kelley. *The Social Psychology of Groups.* New York: John Wiley & Sons, 1959.

Tracy, Brian H. "Bargaining as Trial and Error." In *The Negotiation Process,* edited by I. William Zartman. Beverly Hills: Sage, 1977.

United States Congress, House of Representatives, Committee on Foreign Affairs and Committee on Merchant Marine and Fisheries. *United Nations Security Council Meeting in Panama,* joint committee hearings, 93d Congress, 1st session, April 3, 1973. Washington, D.C.: G.P.O., 1973.

——— Committee on Merchant Marine and Fisheries. *Briefings Concerning Treaty Negotiations and Current Activities of the Panama Canal and Canal Zone,* committee hearing, 93d Congress, 1st session, April 13, 1973. Washington, D.C.: G.P.O., 1973.

——— Subcommittee on Inter-American Affairs of the Committee on Foreign Affairs. *Panama Canal, 1971,* 93d Congress, 1st session, September 1971. Washington, D.C.: G.P.O., 1971.

United States Congress, Senate, Committee on Foreign Relations. *Senate Debate on the Panama Canal Treaties,* 96th Congress, 1st session, February 1979. Washington, D.C.: G.P.O., 1979.

Vance, Cyrus R. *Hard Choices.* New York: Simon & Schuster, 1983.

Vital, David. "The Analysis of Small Power Politics." In *Small States in International Relations,* edited by August Schou and Arne Olav Brundtland. Stockholm: Almqvist & Wiskell, 1971.

Von Neumann, John, and Oskar Morgenstern. *Theory of Games and Economic Behavior*. Princeton: Princeton University Press, 1947.

Waltz, Kenneth. *Theory of International Politics*. Menlo Park, N.J.: Addison Wesley, 1979.

Weeks, Stanley Byron. "United States Defense Policy toward Spain, 1950–1976." Ph.D. dissertation, The American University, 1977.

Wells, Samuel F., Jr. "Sounding the Tocsin: NSC-68 and the Soviet Threat." *International Security* 4 (Fall 1979): 116–38.

Whitaker, Arthur. *Spain and Defense of the West*. New York: Harper & Row, 1961.

Wriggins, W. Howard. "Up for Auction: Malta Bargains with Great Britain." In *The 50% Solution*, edited by I. William Zartman. Garden City, N.Y.: Anchor Press, 1976.

Young, Oran, ed. *Bargaining*. Urbana: University of Illinois Press, 1975.

————. *The Politics of Force: Bargaining in International Crises*. Princeton: Princeton University Press, 1968.

Zartman, I. William. "Negotiation as a Joint Decision-Making Process." In *The Negotiation Process*, edited by I. William Zartman. Beverly Hills: Sage, 1977.

————. "The Political Analysis of Negotiation: How Who Gets What and When." *World Politics* 26 (April 1974): 385–99.

————. *The Politics of Trade Negotiations between Africa and the European Economic Community*. Princeton: Princeton University Press, 1971.

————, ed. *The 50% Solution*. Garden City, N.Y.: Anchor Press, 1976.

————, ed. *The Negotiation Process*. Beverly Hills: Sage, 1977.

Zartman, I. William, and Maureen R. Berman. *The Practical Negotiator*. New Haven: Yale University Press, 1982.

Zeuthen, Frank. *Problems of Monopoly and Economic Warfare*. London: Routledge & Kegan Paul, 1930.

Index